Hook Heritage

Crochet Earring Lesson Book
Written by: A. Redris Bell

DEDICATION

CHAPTERS

- 1. **Introduction to Crochet Earrings**
  - Brief history of crochet earrings
  - Overview of different crochet techniques used in earring making
  - How to read a stitch chart
  - Acronym Key

- 2. **Materials and Tools**
  - Yarn types and weights
  - Crochet hooks and other essential tools
  - Additional embellishments (beads, charms, etc.)

- 3. **Basic Crochet Stitches for Earrings**
  - Slip stitch, chain stitch
  - Single crochet, double crochet, half-double crochet
  - Treble crochet, triple treble crochet, cluster, puff stitch, shell stitch
  - Tunisian crochet
  - Increase and decrease stitches

- 4. **Hoops Tutorials**
  - Puffer Stitch Hoop
  - Bullion Stitch Hoop
  - Flower Hoop
  - Shell Hoop
  - Chandelier Hoop

- **5. Dangle Tutorials**
  - Flower Vine
  - Pineapple Twist
  - Bullion Puff Circle
  - Tassel Doily
  - Leaf - Tunisian crochet

- **6. Finishing Techniques**
  - Blocking and shaping
  - Adding earring findings
  - Securing ends and weaving in yarn tails

- 7. **Troubleshooting Common Issues**
  - Fixing tension problems
  - Dealing with yarn splitting
  - Adjusting patterns for different yarn weights

DEDICATION

Embark on a nostalgic journey as I recollect the vivid memories of my childhood—a curious little boy enchanted by the rhythmic dance of my great-grandmother's crochet hook. I can still envision her seated on the red couch, engrossed in the drama of "Days of Our Lives," effortlessly transforming skeins of yarn into cozy blankets that enveloped our family and community.

In a defining moment, my great-grandmother extended an invitation, offering me a yarn and hook, initiating me into the enchanting world of crochet. Though I may not have completed an entire blanket, the sheer joy found in crafting a simple square ignited a passion for creation that would stay with me throughout the years.

Fast forward 30 years, and that little boy has evolved into a multi-medium artist. Finding myself weary of polymer clay and resins, a serendipitous encounter with my grandmother's photograph breathed new life into my artistic spirit. Inspired by her enduring legacy, I reached for the same hook, not for blankets this time, but for a pair of earrings. Thus began a profound re-connection with the craft.

However, this venture into crochet was unlike the familiar blankets of my childhood. Learning anew, I delved into online references, only to be met with confusing jargon and intricate patterns in silent, swift tutorials. Fueled by the desire to demystify this intricate art, I embarked on writing this book.

Within these pages, discover a treasure trove of instructions, tips, and answers born out of my personal struggles to comprehend the complexities of crochet. In sharing my insights, I hope to illuminate the path for those venturing into the world of crochet, providing a resource that speaks the language of passion, patience, and understanding—a legacy inspired by the enduring magic of that red-couched, story-filled room. May this book kindle your own creative flame and make your crochet journey a seamless, joyous adventure.

I dedicate this book to my late great grandmother "Granny"
Cliddie Mae Clark

CHAPTER 1
Introduction to Crochet Earrings

Brief history of crochet earrings

The history of crochet earrings is closely intertwined with the rich and diverse history of crochet itself. Crocheting, as a textile art form, has ancient roots dating back to the early 19th century in Europe. However, crochet earrings specifically gained popularity as a fashionable accessory in more recent times.

Early Influences:

Crocheting has its origins in traditional lace-making techniques, with roots in various cultures, including French, Irish, and Italian needlework. The intricate patterns and delicate craftsmanship of these early crocheted pieces laid the foundation for the development of crochet as a versatile craft.

One of the earliest instances of crochet can be found in the Middle East, where skilled artisans engaged in "needle binding." This ancient technique, resembling crochet, utilized a single-eyed needle to create intricate looped stitches. Evidence of needle binding has been discovered in archaeological finds dating back to the 11th century in Egypt.

Italian twisted awe

Egyptian sock

Rise in Popularity:

The mid-20th century saw a surge in the popularity of crochet as a domestic craft and a means of creative expression. As women engaged in various needlework activities, the versatility of crochet became evident. Crochet enthusiasts started experimenting with different forms and patterns, giving rise to the creation of crochet jewelry, including earrings.

Bohemian and Hippie Movement:

During the 1960s and 1970s, the bohemian and hippie movements embraced handmade crafts as a form of self-expression and rejection of mass-produced goods. Crochet, with its artisanal and free-spirited nature, became a favored medium for creating unique and personalized accessories, including earrings. The era's fashion embraced the use of bold colors and unconventional designs, further fueling the popularity of crochet earrings.

Contemporary Trends:

In recent decades, crochet earrings have experienced a resurgence in popularity, thanks in part to the revival of interest in handmade and artisanal products. The DIY (Do It Yourself) culture, bolstered by online platforms and social media, has allowed crafters to share and showcase their creations, contributing to the popularity of crochet earrings as a fashionable and customizable accessory.

Today, crochet earrings come in a myriad of styles, from delicate lace designs to bold and modern geometric shapes. The craft continues to evolve, with contemporary crocheters combining traditional techniques with innovative materials and styles.

Crochet earrings not only reflect the craftsmanship and creativity of the maker but also carry a unique blend of tradition and modernity, making them a distinctive and cherished accessory in the world of handmade jewelry.

African American Influence of Crochet

The history of African American crochet is a rich tapestry that weaves together skill, tradition, and cultural expression. Rooted in a legacy of resilience and creativity, the practice of crochet among African Americans has deep historical roots that have evolved over generations.

Early History:
Enslaved individuals, particularly enslaved African women, demonstrated remarkable skills in various handicrafts, including crochet. Despite the harsh conditions of slavery, these women found ways to express their creativity and create functional items for their communities. While the historical record may not provide extensive details, we can draw insights from various sources and cultural histories.

Types of Crocheted Items:

- Functional Textiles: Enslaved individuals often crocheted practical items such as blankets, hats, shawls, and even bedspreads. These items served dual purposes, providing warmth and comfort while also serving as artistic expressions.

- Household Items: Crocheted items extended to household goods, including pot holders, dishcloths, and baskets. These practical creations showcased the resourcefulness and skill of enslaved women in utilizing available materials.

- Garments: Crocheted garments like shawls and scarves were not only utilitarian but also served as cultural markers, often incorporating traditional patterns and symbols that conveyed cultural identity.

Sources of Yarn:
- Home-Spun Yarn: In many cases, enslaved individuals would have spun their own yarn from materials available to them. This could include cotton, wool, or plant fibers. Spinning wheels or drop spindles might have been used to create yarn from raw materials.
- Rations and Scraps: Enslaved individuals received rations, and while these were often meager, they sometimes included materials like cotton or wool that could be unraveled or repurposed for crocheting. Additionally, scraps from sewing projects or discarded clothing might be used for crochet.
- Resourcefulness: Enslaved individuals were resourceful, making use of whatever materials they could find. This might include repurposing old textiles, unraveling worn-out clothing, or using plant fibers for crocheting.

Cultural Significance:
- Storytelling Through Stitches: Crocheted items held cultural significance, often incorporating symbols and patterns that conveyed stories, traditions, and even coded messages related to freedom and resistance.
- Community Bonding: Enslaved individuals formed tight-knit communities where skills were shared. Crocheting circles provided spaces for women to come together, share stories, and pass down techniques from one generation to the next.
- Spiritual Connection: The act of creating, whether through crocheting or other crafts, also served as a form of spiritual connection. Many enslaved individuals infused their creations with a sense of spirituality and resilience.

While the historical record may not provide a comprehensive account of the crochet practices of enslaved individuals, the surviving artifacts and cultural narratives reflect a profound legacy of creativity, resourcefulness, and cultural expression within the confines of slavery. The ability to transform meager resources into beautiful and meaningful creations stands as a testament to the strength and ingenuity of those who lived through that challenging period of history.

Post-Emancipation:
- Economic Empowerment: After emancipation, crochet became a means of economic empowerment for many African American women. Craftsmanship allowed them to create and sell handmade goods, providing a source of income for their families.

- Storytelling Through Stitches: Crochet in the African American community became a form of storytelling. Many creations, from blankets to garments, carried cultural symbols and meanings, preserving traditions and connecting generations.

Harlem Renaissance:
- Artistic Expression: During the Harlem Renaissance in the early 20th century, crochet gained recognition as an art form. African American artists and intellectuals celebrated handmade crafts, elevating crochet to a form of artistic expression.

Civil Rights Movement:
- Craft as Activism: The Civil Rights Movement saw an intertwining of craft and activism. Crochet circles provided spaces for women to discuss social issues, creating a sense of community and solidarity.

Contemporary Times:
- Cultural Heritage: Today, African American crochet artists continue to draw inspiration from their cultural heritage. Many incorporate traditional patterns, colors, and symbols into contemporary designs, preserving and celebrating their roots.
- Online Communities: The digital age has allowed for the flourishing of online crochet communities where African American crafters share their work, patterns, and stories. This has led to a resurgence of interest in handmade crafts within the community.

Recognition in the Arts:
- Art Galleries and Museums: African American crochet artists have gained recognition in art galleries and museums. Their creations are celebrated not only for their aesthetic appeal but also for the cultural narratives they carry.

Economic Empowerment:
- Small Businesses: Many African American entrepreneurs have turned their crochet skills into successful small businesses, selling handmade items, patterns, and offering crochet workshops. This entrepreneurial spirit continues the tradition of economic empowerment.

The history of African American crochet is intertwined with the broader narrative of African American history. From the challenging times of enslavement to the creative expressions of today, crochet remains a powerful means of storytelling, cultural preservation, and economic empowerment within the African American community. As contemporary artists continue to innovate and celebrate their heritage, the legacy of African American crochet evolves and leaves an indelible mark on the world of fiber arts.

Louisville, Kentucky, church rectory, c1942

Overview of different crochet techniques used in earring making

Here's an overview of different crochet techniques commonly used in earring making:

1. Slip Stitch (sl st):
   - A short and tight stitch, slip stitches are commonly used for joining rounds or creating subtle connections in earring designs.

2. Chain Stitch (ch):
   - The foundation of many crochet projects, chain stitches are often used to create loops for attaching findings or forming the base of various earring designs.

3. Basic Crochet Stitches
   - Single Crochet (sc): A simple stitch that creates a dense fabric. It's often used for solid and sturdy earring designs.

   - Double Crochet (dc): Taller than single crochet, this stitch is great for creating lacy and airy earring patterns.

4. Increasing and Decreasing:
   - Increasing: Adding stitches to create a wider or rounder shape in earring designs.

   - Decreasing: Removing stitches to shape the earring or create interesting patterns.

5. Crochet in the Round:
   - Working in a continuous spiral to create circular or oval-shaped earrings, often used for hoop designs.

6. Filet Crochet:
   - A technique that involves creating open and closed mesh patterns, perfect for achieving delicate and lace-like earring designs.

7. Tunisian Crochet:
   - Combining elements of crochet and knitting, Tunisian crochet creates a dense and textured fabric. It's suitable for creating sturdy and warm earring designs.

8. Lacework:
   - Incorporating intricate lace patterns into earring designs for an elegant and delicate look. Lacework often involves using fine yarn and small crochet hooks.

9. Broomstick Lace:
   - A technique that creates a lacy and openwork pattern resembling the bristles of a broomstick. It's ideal for creating unique and eye-catching earring designs.

10. Color-work:
   - Techniques like tapestry crochet or color changes can be employed to add visual interest and complexity to earring patterns.

11. Bead Crochet:
   - Integrating beads into the crochet work to create embellished and textured earring designs. This technique requires adding beads during the stitching process.

12. Free-form Crochet:
   - A more abstract and artistic approach where crocheters use a variety of stitches and techniques in a less structured manner to create one-of-a-kind earring designs.

Understanding and experimenting with these crochet techniques can open up a world of possibilities for creating diverse and beautiful crochet earrings. The combination of different stitches and methods allows crafters to customize their designs to suit various styles and preferences.

How to read a stitch chart

Reading a crochet stitch chart can be a helpful skill for crocheters, especially when working with complex or intricate patterns. My first encounter with a crochet pattern symbol chart was a mix of excitement and confusion. The intricate combination of symbols, lines, and shapes on the chart initially left me feeling bewildered, like deciphering a secret code.

As a beginner, I struggled to connect the visual representation on paper with the tangible act of crocheting. The various symbols seemed like an abstract language, and interpreting their meaning required a patient unraveling of the pattern's mysteries. However, with persistence and the help of online tutorials, the chart slowly unveiled its secrets, and what once appeared perplexing transformed into a roadmap guiding me through the beautiful world of crochet stitches.

 Overcoming that initial confusion became a rewarding journey, marking the beginning of my understanding and appreciation for the versatile language of crochet pattern charts. I won't be using stitch charts for my tutorials, however this information is valuable to know. Here are step-by-step instructions on how to read a crochet stitch chart:

1. Understand the Symbols:
   - Familiarize yourself with the symbols used in the chart. Common symbols include a filled-in square for single crochet, a T-shape for treble crochet, and lines indicating chains.

2. Identify the Starting Point:
   - Most charts have an arrow or a symbol indicating the starting point. Begin reading the chart from this point.

3. Read Right to Left (for Right-Handed Crocheters):
   - Just as you read written crochet patterns, crochet stitch charts are typically read from right to left. Each row represents a new round or row of crochet.

4. Follow the Rows:
   - Each row in the chart represents a row of stitches in your crochet work. The rows are usually numbered, and you progress from one row to the next.

5. Understand Symbols for Stitches:
   - Different stitches are represented by specific symbols. For example:
     - A filled square might represent a single crochet.
     - A T-shape might represent a treble crochet.
     - Ovals or circles might represent chain stitches.

6. Pay Attention to Repeat Sections:
   - Some charts have sections that are repeated. Look for brackets or other indicators that show where a specific sequence of stitches should be repeated.

7. Check for Additional Notations:
   - Some charts include additional information, such as color changes, special stitches, or notes. These are usually explained in a key or legend provided with the chart.

8. Count Stitches and Rows:
   - Use the chart to count the number of stitches and rows in each section. This helps ensure accuracy in your work.

9. Be Mindful of Turning Chains:
   - Turning chains may be represented by a special symbol or noted in the key. These chains often serve as the starting point for a new row.

10. Practice with Simple Charts:
   - If you're new to reading crochet charts, start with simpler patterns to practice and build your confidence.

11. Use a Color Legend (if applicable):

- If the chart uses different colors to represent different stitches or actions, refer to a color legend or key to understand the meaning of each color.

12. Consult Pattern Instructions:

- In conjunction with the chart, refer to any written pattern instructions that accompany it. The written instructions can provide additional context and guidance.

13. Take Your Time:

- Reading crochet charts may feel overwhelming at first, but with practice, it becomes more intuitive. Take your time to understand each symbol and how it corresponds to a specific crochet stitch.

By following these steps, you can navigate and interpret crochet stitch charts more effectively, allowing you to tackle a broader range of crochet patterns with confidence.

CROCHET STITCH CHART

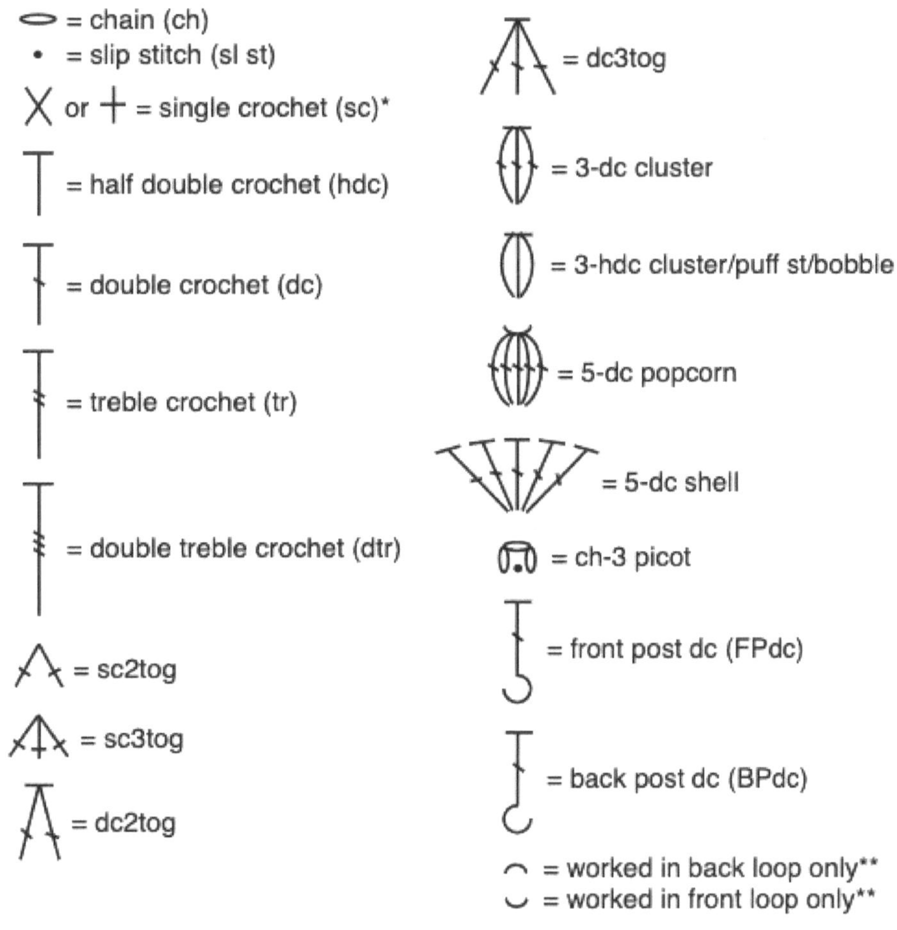

EXAMPLES

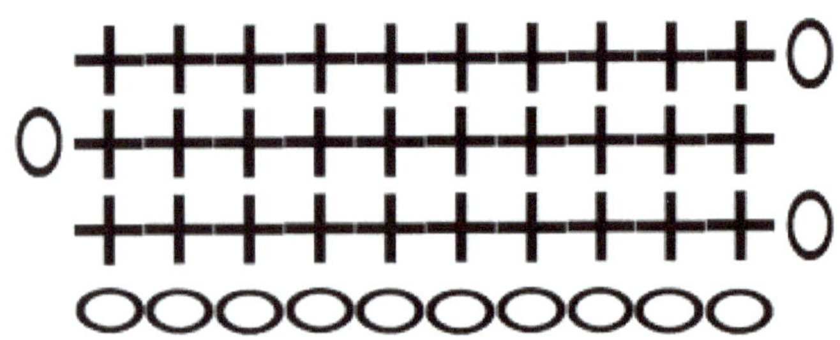

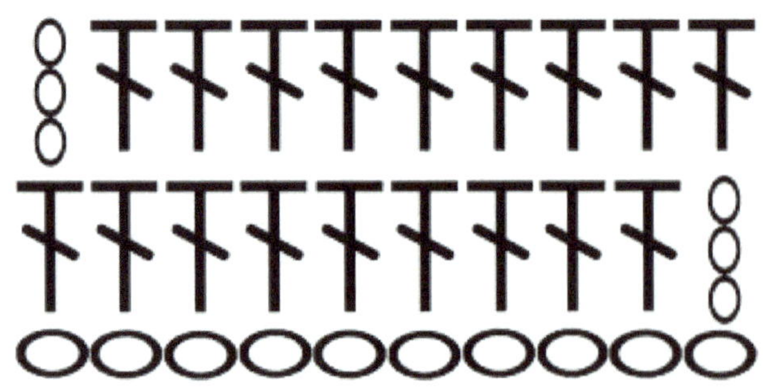

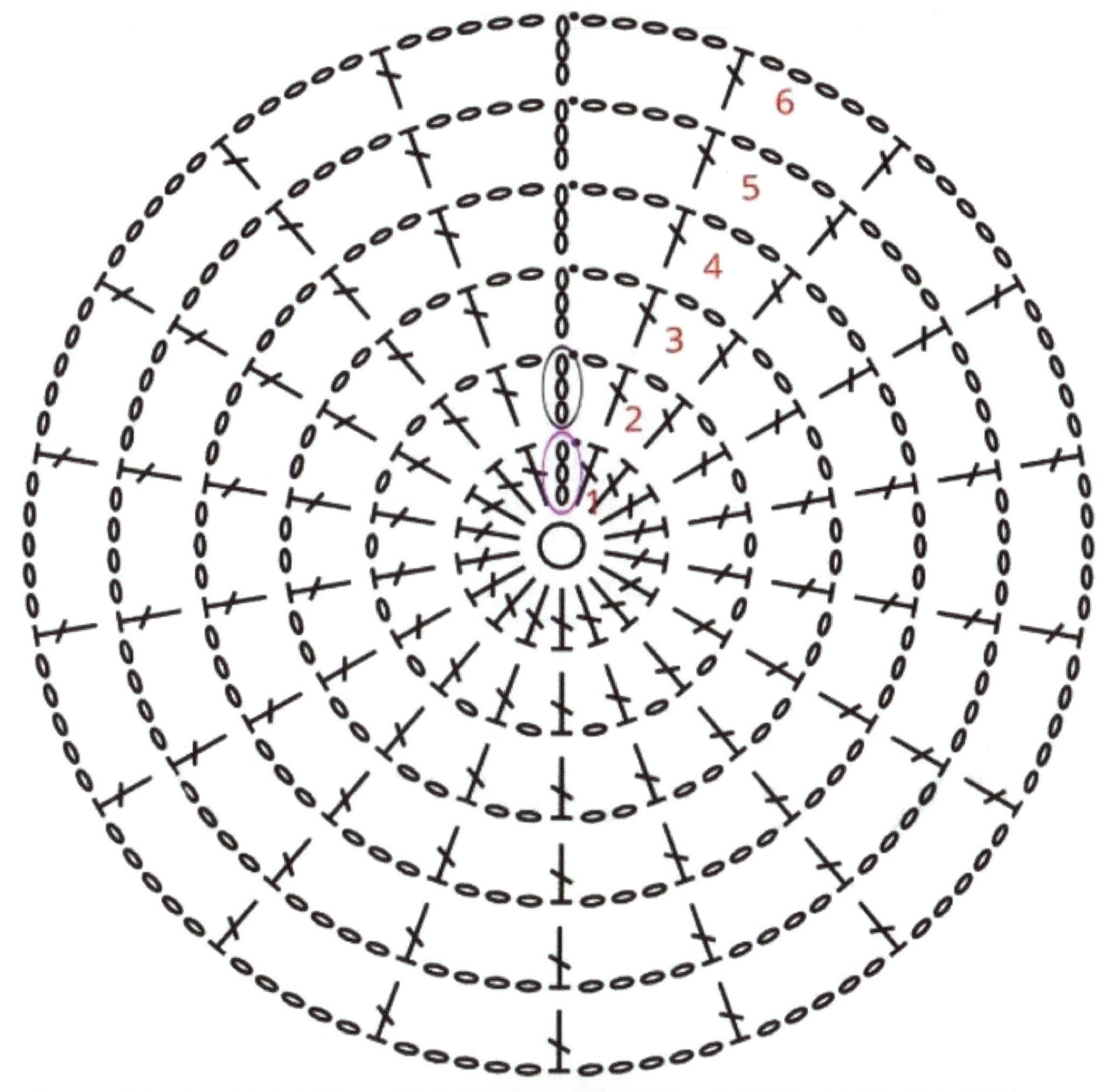

Notice how this chart starts at the ch3 in the purple circle. you will work towards the right. each number represents the row or round. there are 6 rows or rounds in total. this pattern also repeats itself each round with more reps. you can easily convert the size by omitting or adding more rows or rounds.

ROUND 2 READS: CH3 [CHAIN 3], CH1 [CHAIN 1] , DC [DOUBLE CROCHET]. REP 17 [REPEAT 17 TIMES], SLST [SLIP STICH INTO CHAIN 3

I promise once you learn the symbols this is actually easier than written patterns.

Stitch Acronym Key

SLST = Slip Stitch
CH = Chain
SC = Single Crochet
HDC = Half Double Crochet
DC = Double Crochet
SC2TOG = single crochet 2 stitches together
DC2TOG = double crochet 2 stitches together
HDC2TOG = half double crochet 2 stitches together
TR = treble crochet
TR2TOG = treble crochet 2 stitches together
TRTR = triple treble crochet
CL = cluster
PC = popcorn stitch
PS or **PUFF** = puff stitch
SH = shell

Instruction Acronym Key

ALT =: alternate
APPROX = approximately
BEG = begin/beginning
BET = between
CH-**SP** = chain space
CONT = continue
DEC = decrease
INC = increase
FL or **FLO** = front loop/front loop only
TCH = turning chain
SK = skip
YO = yarn over
YOH = yarn over hook

Chapter 2:
Materials & Tools

Yarn Types and Weights

Selecting the right yarn for your crochet earrings is a crucial step in achieving the desired look and feel of your creations. Yarn comes in a variety of types and weights, each with its unique characteristics. In this chapter, we will explore the different aspects of yarn, helping you make informed choices for your crochet earring projects.

Yarn labels will give you information like: yarn weight category (light, medium, bulky) yarn weight and yardage. fiber content, such as wool or cotton. Suggested needle size for knitting or hook size for crocheting to achieve the best results with the yarn.

Recommended gauge information (number of stitches and rows per inch or centimeter) for a standardized 4x4 inch (10x10 cm) swatch. This helps ensure your project matches the intended size. Understanding the information on a yarn label can help you make informed choices based on your project requirements and preferences. Always refer to the label for accurate details about the yarn you're working with.

1. BRAND & YARN NAME
2. WEIGHT CATEGORY
3. WEIGHT
4. YARDAGE
5. GAUGE
6. FIBER CONTENT
7. COLOR AND DYE LOT
8. CARE INSTRUCTIONS

Understanding Yarn Types:

1. Natural Fibers
   - Cotton: Is ideal for lightweight and breathable earrings, cotton yarn is comfortable to wear and comes in various weights.
   - Linen: Is known for its crisp texture, linen yarn adds a rustic touch to earrings and works well for warm-weather accessories.

2. Animal Fibers:
   - Wool: A classic choice, wool yarn offers warmth and elasticity. Consider it for fall and winter-themed earrings.
   - Alpaca: Soft and luxurious, alpaca yarn adds a touch of elegance to delicate earring designs.

3. Synthetic Fibers:
   - Acrylic: Budget-friendly and available in a wide range of colors, acrylic yarn is great for experimenting with different shades in your earrings.
   - Nylon: Durable and resilient, nylon yarn is suitable for creating sturdy earrings with added strength.

4. Blended Fibers:
   - Wool Blends: Combining the warmth of wool with other fibers like acrylic or nylon, wool blends offer a balance of comfort and durability.
   - Cotton Blends: Blending cotton with other fibers results in yarn that combines breathability with added structure.

WOOL
Wool is the most widely used fiber in knitting and for good reason. It's highly insulating, breathable, and warm. However, it can cause allergic reactions and be itchy for some people.

CASHMERE
Cashmere is known for its softness and fluffiness. The fibers are delicate and become even softer with use. However, it is a luxury fabric that is more expensive than wool. Additionally, cashmere is not as strong .

MOHIAR
Mohair yarn is popular for several reasons, including its shiny, lightweight, & fluffy texture. In addition to being warm, it is also highly durable. It's often combined with other fibers to increase weight and strength.

COTTON
Cotton is a plant-based fiber that is strong, absorbent, and inexpensive. Cotton is ideal for well-defined stitch-work, and it does not cause skin irritation. However, it is less elastic compared to other types of yarn.

SILK
Silk yarns are known for their strength, lustrous shine, and smooth texture. They are lightweight and breathable, making them an ideal choice for a summer fabric.

LINEN
Linen is a type of plant-based fiber that is strong light & absorbent. However, it wrinkles easily. Though on the other hand, linen is much more elastic than cotton and is better for blocking.

ACRYLIC
Understanding Acrylic Fiber Properties
Acrylic is an artificial fiber known for its excellent heat retention. It is a robust and affordable option, but not as breathable or absorbent as natural fibers.

POLYESTER
Polyester is a robust synthetic yarn that can be machine washed. It is typically blended with other fibers to enhance its strength, durability, and reduce shrinkage. However, when used alone, it may feel rough and scratchy.

Deciphering Yarn Weights:

Yarn weight refers to the thickness or diameter of the yarn strand and plays a significant role in determining the drape, texture, and overall appearance of your crochet earrings.

1. Lace Weight (0):
   - Delicate and fine, lace weight yarn is suitable for creating intricate lace patterns in lightweight and ethereal earrings.

2. Fingering Weight (1):
   - Often used for delicate projects, fingering weight yarn is great for lightweight and dainty earrings.

3. Sport Weight (2):
   - A versatile weight, sport weight yarn works well for a variety of earring styles, offering a good balance between drape and structure.

4. Worsted Weight (4):
   - The most common weight, worsted weight yarn is suitable for a wide range of earring designs, providing a balance of durability and comfort.

5. Bulky Weight (5):
   - Bulky weight yarn adds thickness and warmth, making it ideal for bold and chunky earring styles.

6. Super Bulky Weight (6):
   - Perfect for quick projects, super bulky weight yarn creates bold statement earrings with a substantial and cozy feel.

Considerations When Choosing Yarn:

1. Earring Design:
   - Consider the intricacy of your design. Fine details may be better suited to thinner yarn, while bold, structural designs may benefit from thicker yarn.

2. Season and Climate:
   - Think about the weather. Light and breathable yarns like cotton are great for warm seasons, while wool may be more suitable for colder months.

3. Color Availability:
   - Some yarn types offer a broader spectrum of colors. Consider the color range available in the yarn you choose to achieve the desired aesthetic.

4. Budget and Accessibility:
   - Evaluate your budget and the availability of yarn in your local stores. Affordable and accessible options can make your earring projects more sustainable.

5. Texture and Feel:
   - Think about the texture you want for your earrings. Some yarns have a smooth finish, while others may have a textured or fuzzy appearance.

6. Experimentation:
   - Don't be afraid to experiment with different yarn types and weights. Mix and match to discover unique combinations that enhance your crochet earring creations.

By understanding the characteristics of various yarn types and weights, you empower yourself to make informed decisions that align with your creative vision. Whether you're crafting delicate lace earrings or bold, chunky designs, the right yarn choice can elevate your projects to new heights.

Crochet Hooks and Essential Tools

Crochet hooks and other tools are the foundation of every crochet project, influencing the ease of your work and the final result. In this section, we will explore the different types of crochet hooks and essential tools, as well as how to use them effectively.

1. Materials:
- Metal: Durable and smooth, metal hooks are widely used and come in various finishes.

- Plastic: Lightweight and budget-friendly, plastic hooks are comfortable for extended use.

- Wood: Warm to the touch, wooden hooks provide a comfortable grip and are suitable for those who prefer a natural feel.

2. Sizes:
- Crochet hooks come in various sizes, denoted by letters, numbers, or millimeters. The size influences the gauge and the overall size of your stitches.

3. Handle Styles:
- In-line: The throat and shaft of the hook align, providing a consistent loop size.

- Tapered: The throat gradually widens, allowing for smoother yarn transitions.

4. Ergonomic Hooks:
- Designed with comfort in mind, ergonomic hooks have larger handles to reduce hand strain during extended crochet sessions.

5. Interchangeable Hooks:
- Some sets offer interchangeable hook heads, allowing you to switch between sizes on a single handle.

6. How to Use:
- Hold the hook like a pencil or a knife, choosing the grip that feels most comfortable.

- Insert the hook into the desired stitch from front to back, catching the working yarn with the hook.

- Yarn over the hook and pull a loop through the stitch

- Continue to yarn over and pull through loops according to the stitch pattern.

Other Essential Tools:

1. Yarn Needles (Tapestry Needles):
- Used for weaving in ends and sewing together crochet pieces. Choose a needle with a large eye for easy threading.

2. Scissors:
- A sharp pair of scissors is essential for cutting yarn cleanly. Keep them in your crochet kit for on-the-go projects.

3. Stitch Markers:
- Mark specific stitches or rounds to keep track of your progress. They come in various forms, including locking, split-ring, or removable markers.

4. Measuring Tape:
- Measure your work and check gauge with a flexible measuring tape. Ensure accuracy in sizing for garments and accessories.

Tips for Effective Tool Use:

- **Maintain Tension:**
    - Keep a consistent tension on the yarn for even stitches.

- **Experiment with Grip:**
    - Try different ways of holding your crochet hook to find the most comfortable grip for you.

- **Use Stitch Markers Wisely:**
    - Place stitch markers strategically, such as at the beginning of rounds or to mark specific stitch patterns.

- **Check Gauge Regularly:**
    - Verify your gauge against the pattern requirements to ensure the correct sizing of your project.

- **Invest in Quality Tools:**
    - Quality crochet hooks and tools can make a significant difference in your crafting experience.

By understanding the characteristics of different crochet hooks and essential tools, you can enhance your efficiency and enjoyment of the crochet process. Experiment with various styles and find the tools that complement your personal crochet style.

CHAPTER 3:
Basic Crochet Stitches for Earrings

Slip stitch, chain stitch

Let's go through detailed instructions for two fundamental crochet stitches: slip stitch and chain stitch.

Slip Stitch (sl st):

Step 1: Insert the Hook:

  - Insert the crochet hook into the specified stitch or space.

Step 2: Yarn Over:

  - Yarn over the hook from back to front.

Step 3: Pull Through:

  - Pull the yarn through both the stitch and the loop on the hook. This creates a slip stitch.

Step 4: Repeat:

  - Repeat steps 1-3 as needed. Slip stitches are often used for joining, creating a smooth edge, or moving the yarn across the work without adding height.

Tips:
 - Slip stitches are usually not counted as a stitch in a pattern unless otherwise specified.
 - Maintain a relaxed tension to make it easier to insert the hook into stitches.

Chain Stitch (ch):

Step 1: Create a Slip Knot:
   - Start by creating a slip knot. Make a loop with the yarn, tuck the end through, and pull tight.

Step 2: Insert the Hook:
   - Insert the crochet hook into the slip knot.

Step 3: Yarn Over:
   - Yarn over the hook from back to front.

Step 4: Pull Through:
   - Pull the yarn through the slip knot, creating a new loop on the hook.

Step 5: Repeat:
   - Repeat steps 2-4 to create additional chain stitches. The number of chains you make depends on your pattern.

Tips:
   - Practice creating even and consistent chains for a polished look in your projects.
   - The first chain in a row often serves as a turning chain to bring the yarn to the correct height for the next row.

Common Uses:
   - Foundation Chain: The starting row of many crochet projects.
   - Turning Chains: Used to transition between rows.
   - Decorative Elements: Chains can be used to create loops, laces, or other decorative features.

By mastering the slip stitch and chain stitch, you lay the foundation for various crochet projects. These stitches are the building blocks for more complex stitches and patterns. With practice, you'll develop a smooth and consistent technique, allowing you to confidently tackle a wide range of crochet projects.

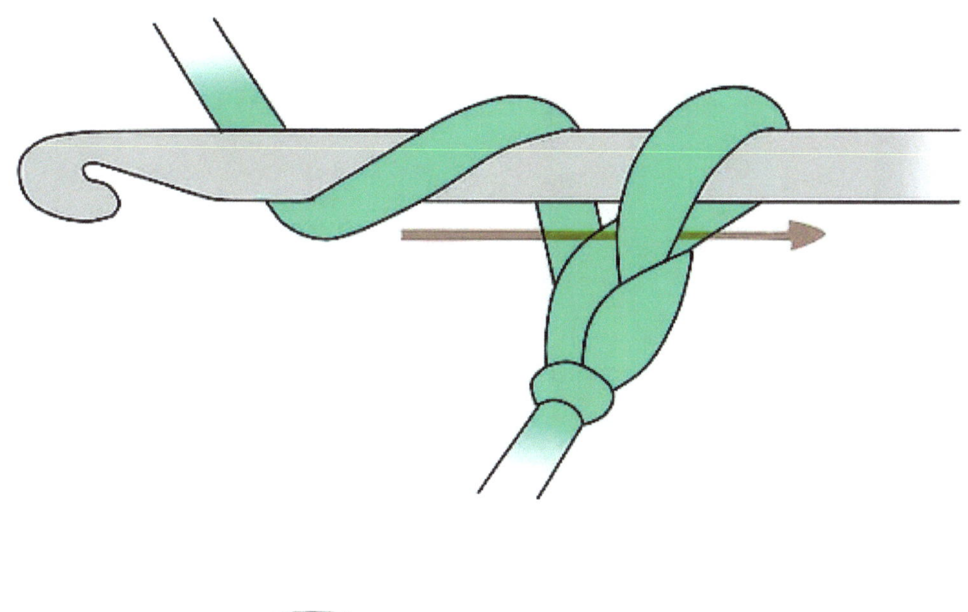

chain (ch)

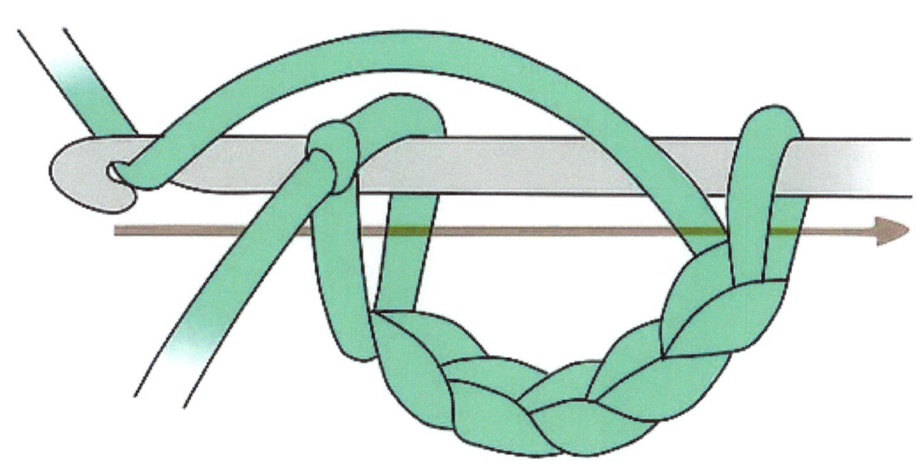

slip stitch (sl st)

Single crochet, half double crochet, double crochet

Single crochet is the shortest of the basic crochet stitches, creating a fabric that is closely packed and has minimal height. This characteristic makes it suitable for projects that require a sturdy and firm structure.

The single crochet pattern produces a smooth and uniform surface on both sides of the fabric. This creates a neat and cohesive appearance without much texture. Unlike taller stitches, such as half double crochet or double crochet, there are minimal gaps between single crochet stitches. This results in a fabric with little to no visible space between the stitches.

Single Crochet:

Step 1: Starting Chain
   - Begin by creating a foundation chain of the desired length.

Step 2: Inserting the Hook
   - Insert your crochet hook into the second chain from the hook. This skipped chain counts as the first single crochet.

Step 3: Yarn Over and Pull Up a Loop
   - Yarn over (wrap the yarn over the hook from back to front) and pull up a loop through the chain stitch. You now have two loops on the hook.

Step 4: Yarn Over and Pull Through Both Loops
   - Yarn over again and pull through both loops on the hook. This completes one single crochet stitch.

Step 5: Repeat
   - Continue this process in each chain across the row. When you reach the end, chain one and turn your work. Repeat these steps for subsequent rows.

Half double crochet allows for the incorporation of colors, making it suitable for colorwork and stripe patterns. The distinct Vs and reduced gaps provide a canvas for showcasing different colors in an aesthetically pleasing manner.

a half double crochet pattern combines the best of both single and double crochet, offering a versatile and visually appealing option for crochet projects. Its balanced height, reduced gaps, and ease of execution make it a favorite among crocheters for a wide range of applications.

Half-Double Crochet:

Step 1: Starting Chain
  - Create a foundation chain of the desired length.

Step 2: Yarn Over and Insert the Hook
  - Yarn over and insert the hook into the third chain from the hook.

Step 3: Yarn Over and Pull Up a Loop
  - Yarn over and pull up a loop through the chain stitch. You now have three loops on the hook.

Step 4: Yarn Over and Pull Through All Loops
  - Yarn over once more and pull through all three loops on the hook. This completes one half-double crochet stitch.

Step 5: Repeat
  - Continue these steps in each chain across the row. Chain one at the end of the row and turn your work. Repeat for subsequent rows.

Practice these basic crochet stitches to build a solid foundation for more complex projects. As you become more comfortable with these fundamental stitches, you'll be ready to explore and experiment with various crochet patterns and techniques.

When worked in rows, double crochet stitches create V-shaped columns. Each V represents an individual double crochet stitch. The stacked Vs form a visually appealing pattern. On the front side of the fabric, you'll notice horizontal bars running through each double crochet stitch. These bars contribute to the textured appearance of the pattern.

On the back side of the fabric, you'll see vertical lines corresponding to each double crochet stitch. This is a distinctive feature of the stitch and helps create a reversible fabric.

Double Crochet:

Step 1: Starting Chain
  - Create a foundation chain, typically a multiple of two, plus two extra chains.

Step 2: Yarn Over and Insert the Hook
  - Yarn over and insert the hook into the third chain from the hook.

Step 3: Yarn Over and Pull Up a Loop
  - Yarn over and pull up a loop through the chain stitch. You now have three loops on the hook.

Step 4: Yarn Over and Pull Through Two Loops
  - Yarn over and pull through the first two loops on the hook. You have two loops remaining.

Step 5: Yarn Over and Pull Through Remaining Loops
  - Yarn over once more and pull through the remaining two loops. This completes one double crochet stitch.

Step 6: Repeat
  - Continue these steps in each chain across the row. Chain two at the end of the row and turn your work. Repeat for subsequent rows.

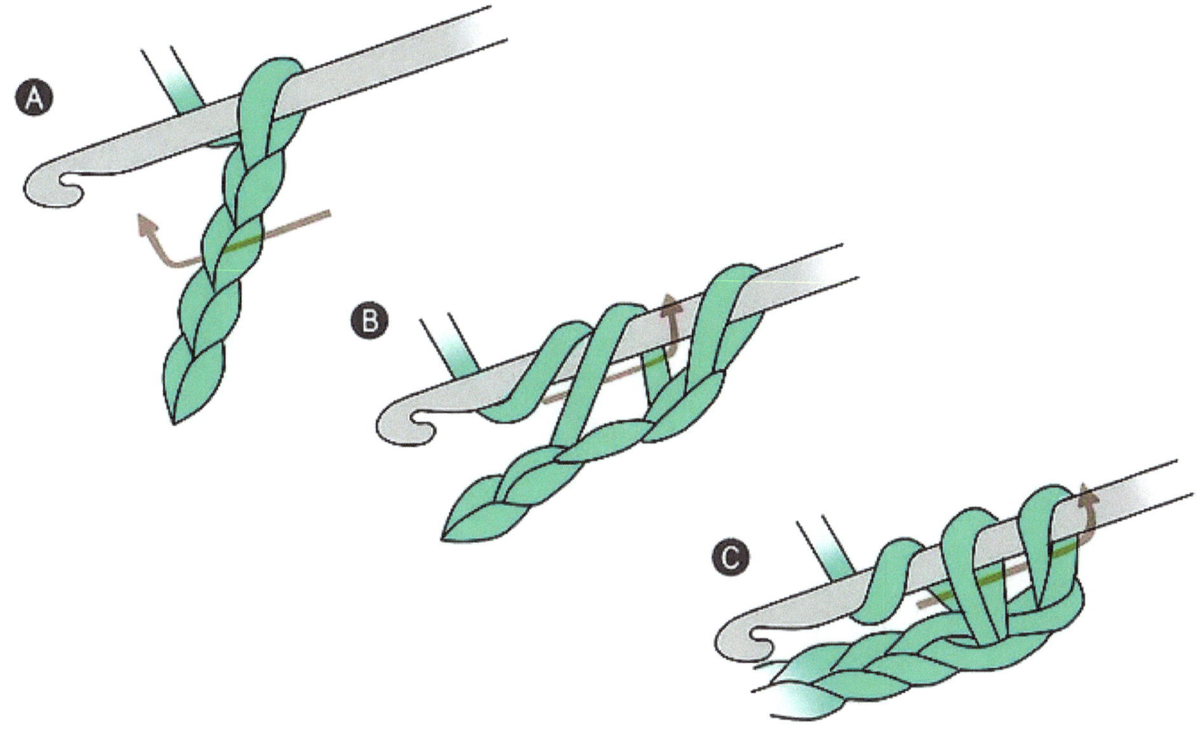

X or $+$ single crochet (sc)

hieght of crochet stiches

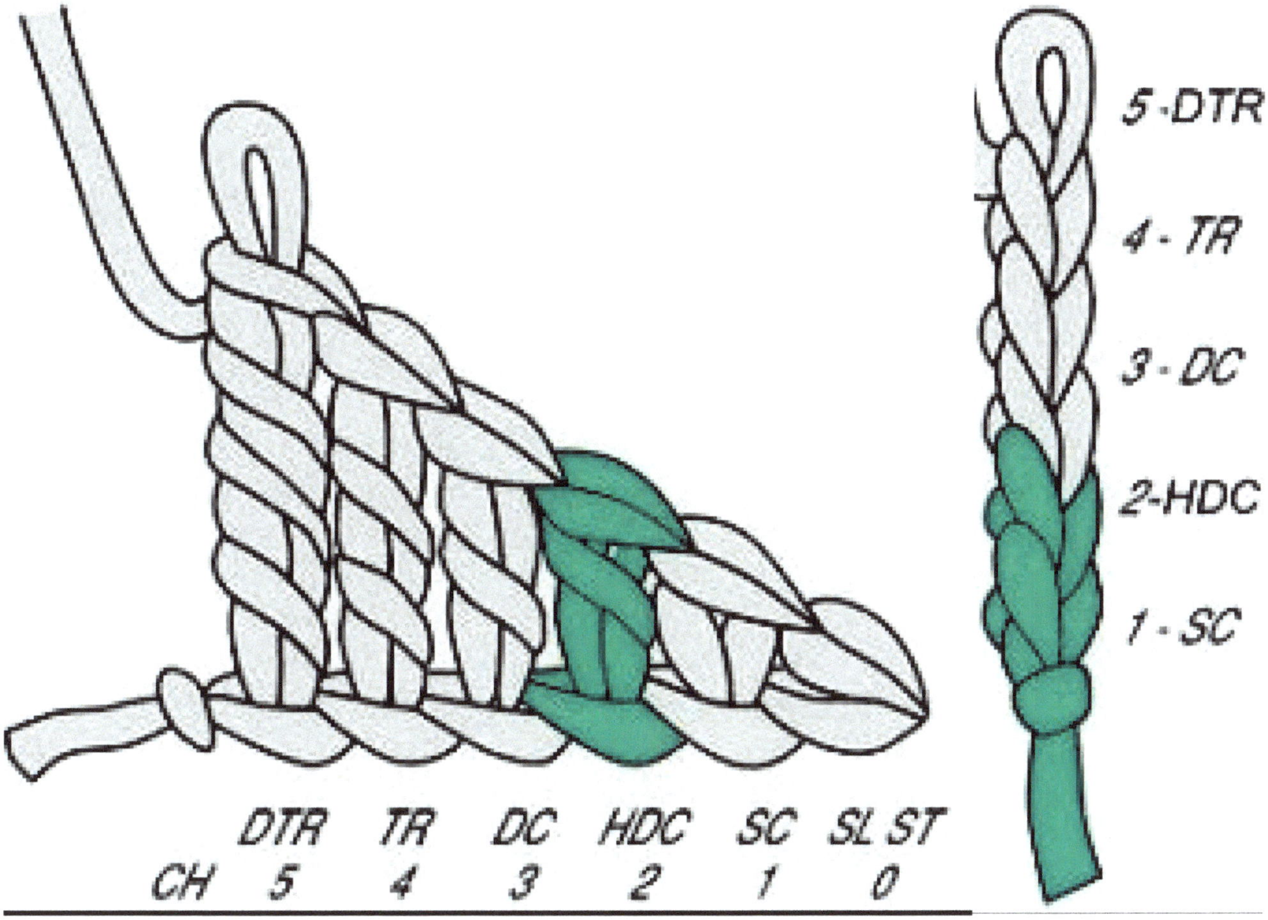

Treble crochet, triple treble crochet, cluster, puff stitch, shell stitch

A treble crochet pattern showcases a distinctive and elongated stitch that adds a sense of openness and grace to the fabric. Treble crochet is notably tall, creating a lacy and open appearance in the fabric. It is one of the tallest basic crochet stitches, taller than both double crochet and half double crochet.

The elongated nature of the treble crochet imparts a lacy appearance to the fabric, making it well-suited for lightweight and breathable projects such as shawls, doilies, or openwork garments.

Treble Crochet (Tr):

Step 1: Yarn Over Twice (YO):
   - Begin with a yarn over twice, wrapping the yarn around the hook two times.

Step 2: Insert the Hook:
   - Insert the hook into the desired stitch or space.

Step 3: Yarn Over and Pull Up a Loop:
   - Yarn over and pull up a loop. You now have four loops on the hook.

Step 4: Yarn Over and Pull Through Two Loops:
   - Yarn over and pull through the first two loops. You have three loops remaining on the hook.

Step 5: Yarn Over and Pull Through Two Loops Again:
   - Yarn over and pull through the next two loops. You have two loops left on the hook.

Step 6: Yarn Over and Pull Through the Final Two Loops:
   - Yarn over one last time and pull through the remaining two loops. This completes one treble crochet stitch.

The triple treble crochet, with its elongated stitches, introduces a touch of elegance to the world of crochet, making it particularly well-suited for column-style knitting. This unique stitch imparts a captivating grace to your creations, forming beautiful straight lines that add a sophisticated dimension to your projects.

When it comes to striped pieces, especially those involving more than one color, the triple treble crochet truly shines. Its height and elongated structure create striking visual appeal in alternating hues, resulting in a dynamic interplay of colors. Whether you're fashioning scarves, blankets, or other multi-colored masterpieces, the triple treble crochet enhances the beauty of each stripe, providing a canvas for vibrant and eye-catching designs.

So, if you're aiming for projects with a refined vertical aesthetic or diving into the world of captivating stripes, the triple treble crochet is a versatile and valuable addition to your repertoire. Let this stitch be your guide as you embark on creating visually stunning, column-style crochet pieces that showcase the artistry of the triple treble.

Triple Treble Crochet (Trtr):

Step 1: Yarn Over Four Times (YO):
  - Start with a yarn over four times, wrapping the yarn around the hook four times.

Step 2: Insert the Hook:
  - Insert the hook into the desired stitch or space.

Step 3: Yarn Over and Pull Up a Loop:
  - Yarn over and pull up a loop. You now have six loops on the hook.

Step 4: Yarn Over and Pull Through Two Loops:
  - Yarn over and pull through the first two loops. Repeat this step until only one loop remains on the hook. This completes one triple treble crochet stitch.

My grandmother's favored crochet technique for making blankets centered around the cluster stitch, now affectionately known as the "granny stitch." It's the very stitch she passed down to me, and I can recognize it anywhere.

This stitch, a beautiful amalgamation of clusters, holds a special place in my heart. Ideal for crafting perfect baby blankets, cozy throws, charming pillowcases, or even expansive bedspreads, it lends itself seamlessly to a variety of projects. My grandmother, a master in her craft, typically worked her wonders in no more than two or three colors, showcasing the timeless simplicity and versatility of the granny stitch.

Cluster Stitch:

Step 1: Yarn Over (YO):
   - Yarn over before inserting the hook into the specified stitch or space.

Step 2: Insert the Hook:
   - Insert the hook into the designated stitch or space.

Step 3: Yarn Over and Pull Up a Loop:
   - Yarn over and pull up a loop. You now have three loops on the hook.

Step 4: Repeat:
   - Yarn over and pull through the first two loops on the hook, leaving two loops on the hook. Repeat steps 1-4 until you have a specified number of loops on the hook.

Step 5: Yarn Over and Pull Through All Loops:
   - After creating the desired number of loops, yarn over and pull through all loops on the hook. This completes one cluster stitch.

A puff stitch crochet pattern is characterized by its plush, three-dimensional texture that creates soft, rounded clusters on the fabric. Puff stitches are often worked to form rounded shapes, resembling small, plush orbs on the fabric. The stitches are designed to gather the yarn and create a puffed effect, adding depth and visual interest to the pattern.

Puff stitches can be arranged in various ways to create diverse designs. Whether worked in rows, rounds, or as part of more intricate stitch patterns, puff stitches offer versatility in design possibilities Puff stitches can be combined with other crochet stitches to create intricate patterns and textures. Whether worked alongside simpler stitches or as part of more complex stitch combinations, puff stitches can add a touch of luxury to a variety of projects.

Puff Stitch:

Step 1: Yarn Over (YO):
  - Yarn over before inserting the hook into the specified stitch or space.

Step 2: Insert the Hook:
  - Insert the hook into the designated stitch or space.

Step 3: Yarn Over and Pull Up a Loop:
  - Yarn over and pull up a loop. You now have three loops on the hook.

Step 4: Repeat:
  - Repeat steps 1-3 for the specified number of times, creating multiple loops on the hook.

Step 5: Yarn Over and Pull Through All Loops:
  - After creating the desired number of loops, yarn over and pull through all loops on the hook. This completes one puff stitch.

A shell stitch crochet pattern is a delightful and decorative motif that creates a series of fan-like or scalloped shapes, resembling shells. The shell stitch produces scalloped edges along the fabric. These scallops are formed by the repeating pattern of stitches, usually worked in the same stitch or space, which results in a curved or wavy edge reminiscent of seashells.

Shell stitch patterns provide opportunities for color experimentation. Each shell can be worked in a different color, creating a vibrant and visually appealing result. Color changes can accentuate the scalloped edges and enhance the overall pattern.

The repeated use of shell stitches creates a textured fabric with a three-dimensional quality. The shells add depth and interest to the surface of the project, making it visually engaging.

Shell Stitch:

Step 1: Work Multiple Stitches in the Same Space:
  - Shell stitches typically consist of multiple stitches (such as double crochet, treble crochet, or other stitches) worked into the same stitch or space.

Step 2: Yarn Over (YO) and Insert Hook:
  - Begin with a yarn over (or as specified in the pattern) and insert the hook into the designated stitch or space.

Step 3: Complete the Stitches:
  - Work the specified number of stitches into the same space.

Step 4: Repeat:
  - Repeat steps 1-3 for each shell stitch in the row or round.

These advanced crochet stitches add intricate details and texture to your projects. As you practice, pay attention to your tension and the specific instructions in your patterns to achieve the desired results. Enjoy the creative process!

Tunisian Crochet

Tunisian crochet is a unique and versatile technique that combines elements of both crochet and knitting. Also known as Afghan crochet, it creates a fabric with a beautiful, textured appearance.

The most prominent feature of Tunisian crochet is the formation of vertical columns of stitches. These columns extend from the foundation row to the final row of the project, giving the fabric a striking appearance.

Materials:

- Yarn suitable for Tunisian crochet.
- Tunisian crochet hook (longer than regular crochet hooks).
- Yarn needle for weaving the loose ends.

Basic Tunisian Crochet Stitch (Tunisian Simple Stitch):

Step 1: Foundation:
  - Start with a foundation chain of desired length. The number of chains depends on your project.

Step 2: Forward Pass (Right to Left):
  - Insert the hook from right to left under the back vertical bar of the second chain from the hook. Yarn over and pull up a loop. Leave this loop on the hook.
  - Repeat this process, inserting the hook under the back vertical bar of each chain across the row. You will have loops on the hook equal to the number of chains in your foundation.

Step 3: Return Pass (Left to Right):
  - Yarn over and pull through one loop on the hook. This creates a chain.
  - Yarn over and pull through two loops - Repeat this across the row until only one loop remains on the hook.

Step 4: Repeat:
  - Repeat the forward and return passes for each row. Tunisian Simple Stitch creates a dense and textured fabric.

Tunisian Crochet Stitch Variations:

1. Tunisian Knit Stitch (TKS):
   - Insert the hook between the front and back vertical bars of the stitch, yarn over, and pull up a loop. Complete the return pass as usual.

2. Tunisian Purl Stitch (TPS):
   - Bring the yarn to the front of the work, insert the hook from right to left under the front vertical bar, yarn over, and pull up a loop. Return pass is the same as for TKS.

3. Increasing:
   - Work two stitches into the same space, either by inserting the hook under two vertical bars or by using another increase method.

4. Decreasing:
   - Insert the hook under two or more vertical bars at once and complete the stitch as usual.

5. Closing Rows:
   - To finish a project or close a row, simply work a slip stitch through the next vertical bar and the loop on the hook.

Tips for Tunisian Crochet:

1. Maintain Tension:
   - Keep a consistent tension to create an even fabric.

2. Experiment with Hook Sizes:
   - Tunisian crochet often requires a larger hook than regular crochet. Experiment to achieve the desired drape.

3. Explore Patterns:
   - Tunisian crochet patterns may combine different stitches and techniques. Follow instructions carefully and practice.

4. Decreasing:
   - Insert the hook under two or more vertical bars at once and complete the stitch as usual.

5. Closing Rows:
   - To finish a project or close a row, simply work a slip stitch through the next vertical bar and the loop on the hook.

Tips for Tunisian Crochet:

1. Maintain Tension:
   - Keep a consistent tension to create an even fabric.

2. Experiment with Hook Sizes:
   - Tunisian crochet often requires a larger hook than regular crochet. Experiment to achieve the desired drape.

3. Explore Patterns:
   - Tunisian crochet patterns may combine different stitches and techniques. Follow instructions carefully and practice.

4. Blocking:
   - Block your finished Tunisian crochet projects for a neater appearance.

5. Have Patience:
   - Tunisian crochet may feel different at first, but with practice, it becomes an enjoyable and rewarding technique.

As you practice Tunisian crochet, you'll discover its unique qualities and find ways to incorporate it into various projects, from scarves and blankets to more intricate designs.

Increase and decrease stitches

Increasing and decreasing stitches in crochet are essential techniques for shaping your projects. Let's explore detailed instructions for both increasing and decreasing stitches.

Increasing Stitches:

1. Single Crochet Increase (sc inc):
   - Work two single crochet stitches into the same stitch or space.

Step 1: Insert the Hook:
   - Insert your hook into the specified stitch or space.

Step 2: Single Crochet:
   - Yarn over and pull up a loop.
   - Yarn over and pull through both loops on the hook.
   - Repeat these two steps in the same stitch or space.

2. Double Crochet Increase (dc inc):
   - Work two double crochet stitches into the same stitch or space.

Step 1: Insert the Hook:
   - Insert your hook into the specified stitch or space.

Step 2: Double Crochet:
   - Yarn over and pull up a loop.
   - Yarn over and pull through the first two loops on the hook.
   - Yarn over again and pull through the remaining two loops on the hook.
   - Repeat these three steps in the same stitch or space.

3. Cluster Increase:

 - Work multiple stitches (such as double crochet or treble crochet) into the same stitch or space.

Step 1: Insert the Hook:
   - Insert your hook into the specified stitch or space.

Step 2: Complete the Stitches:
   - Work the specified number of stitches into the same stitch or space.

Decreasing Stitches:

1. Single Crochet Decrease (sc dec):
   - Combine two single crochet stitches into one.

Step 1: Insert the Hook:
   - Insert your hook into the first stitch.

Step 2: Yarn Over and Pull Up a Loop:
   - Yarn over and pull up a loop.

Step 3: Insert the Hook into the Next Stitch:
   - Insert your hook into the next stitch.

Step 4: Yarn Over and Pull Up a Loop:
   - Yarn over and pull up a loop.

Step 5: Yarn Over and Pull Through All Loops:
   - Yarn over and pull through all three loops on the hook.

2. Double Crochet Decrease (dc dec):
 - Combine two double crochet stitches into one.

Step 1: Yarn Over and Insert the Hook:
 - Yarn over and insert your hook into the first stitch.
 - Yarn over and pull up a loop.

Step 3: Yarn Over and Pull Through Two Loops:
 - Yarn over and pull through the first two loops on the hook.

Step 4: Yarn Over and Insert the Hook into the Next Stitch:
 - Yarn over and insert your hook into the next stitch.

Step 5: Yarn Over and Pull Up a Loop:
   - Yarn over and pull up a loop.

Step 6: Yarn Over and Pull Through Two Loops:
   - Yarn over and pull through the first two loops on the hook.

Step 7: Yarn Over and Pull Through All Loops:
   - Yarn over and pull through all three loops on the hook.

3. Cluster Decrease:
   - Work multiple stitches together, reducing the number of stitches.

Step 1: Insert the Hook:
   - Insert your hook into the specified stitch or space.

Step 2: Complete the Stitches:
 - Work the specified number of stitches into the same stitch or space.

Step 3: Yarn Over and Pull Through All Loops:
   - Yarn over and pull through all the loops on the hook.

Tips for Increasing and Decreasing:

1. Follow Pattern Instructions:
  - Always follow the specific pattern instructions for increasing and decreasing. Different patterns may use different techniques.

2. Maintain Consistent Tension:
  - Keep a consistent tension throughout your work to achieve even stitches.

3. Count Your Stitches:
  - Regularly count your stitches to ensure you are on track with the pattern.

4. Practice on a Swatch:
  - Practice increasing and decreasing on a swatch before incorporating these techniques into a larger project.

Mastering the art of increasing and decreasing stitches allows you to create projects with the desired shape and structure. Whether you're working on garments, amigurumi, or accessories, these techniques are valuable tools in your crochet skill set.

CHAPTER 4:
HOOP TUTORIALS
PLAYLIST LINK:
https://studio.youtube.com/playlist/PLXiUWKmExY82msUBJ11XZVB-8_8ASyQp8/edit
Puffer Stitch Hoop

The central feature of these earrings is the carefully executed puffed stitch, adding depth and dimension to the design. The puffed stitch creates a series of soft, rounded protrusions along the hoop

Accentuating the circumference of the hoop is a delicate picot edge, offering a refined and feminine touch to the overall design. The picot edge consists of small, decorative loops that elegantly fringe the outer edge of the hoop. These dainty loops contribute to the bohemian aesthetic, evoking a sense of free-spirited style and intricate craftsmanship.

The choice of yarn plays a pivotal role in enhancing the beauty of these earrings. Picture a soft, earthy-toned yarn that complements the bohemian theme, allowing the intricate stitches to stand out with a subtle yet captivating allure. The lightweight nature of the yarn ensures that the earrings are comfortable to wear, making them a perfect accessory for any occasion.

Supplies:

- 4 weight cotton yarn
- 40mm Hoop Earrings
- 5mm crochet hook
- Darning Needle

Pattern

ROW 1: SLST, 20 SC AROUND THE HOOP, CH1 - TRN

ROW 2: 20 SC AROUND THE HOOP, CH2 - TRN

ROW 3: 4 LOOP PUFF STITCH, PULL THROUGH PUFF ,SLPST, CH 1, [20x]CH1

ROW 4: SLST+CH3+SLST BETWEEN EACH PUFF , CUT THE YARN AND SLST

You can hide your loose yarn by weaving them into the pattern with a darning needle or crochet hook. It is easier to achieve with a needle.

TIP: when crocheting around the hoop do it from the front. Pull from thread behind the hoop and single crochet through both loops to create the chain along the hoop.

Bullion Stitch Hoop

These unique earrings showcase a mesmerizing single crochet pattern delicately worked within the hoop, creating an intricate web reminiscent of a dream catcher.

The single crochet pattern inside the hoop forms a captivating design, giving the earrings a touch of bohemian elegance. As you gaze upon them, the openwork pattern creates a central void, much like the heart of a dream catcher.

The overall effect is one of grace and charm, making them a perfect accessory for those who appreciate the fusion of crochet artistry and bohemian style. Adorning these earrings is like wearing a piece of handmade magic, each stitch telling a story of creativity and individuality.

Supplies:

- 2 – 40mm Hoop Earrings
- H/8 – 5mm Crochet Hook
- Worsted Weight cotton
- Darning Needle to sew in ends

Pattern:

START WITH A SL ST ON THE HOOK

ROW 1: SLST, 25 SC AROUND HOOP, CH1 TRN

ROW 2: SLST 25 SC AROUND HOOP, CH2 TRN

ROW 3: BULLION ST

 "tape 2 hooks together with the hooks opposite of each other. The end of one hook should almost be enough space to catch
To catch the yarn. Wrap 6 loops around the two hooks. Insert in the next space and pull through. Then slide the yarn over through the loops."

CH1 [25x]

ROW 4: SC+CH3+SC BETWEEN EACH PUFF , CUT THE YARN AND SLST

Flower Hoop

Introducing our captivating handmade Floral hoop earrings, where elegance meets nature's beauty. Crafted with meticulous attention to detail, these earrings boast a design reminiscent of a blooming bouquet of flowers encircling the hoop.

Adorned with delicate crochet flowers, each earring features five charming blooms hanging gracefully around the hoop .

Experience the enchantment of nature and add a touch of whimsical charm to your ensemble with our Floral hoop earrings. Perfect for both casual outings and special occasions, these earrings are sure to make a statement wherever you go.

Elevate your accessory game and embrace the beauty of handmade craftsmanship with our exquisite Floral hoop earrings.

FLORAL HOOP VIDEO TUTORIAL

https://youtu.be/Kk5gAmJXNXo?si=dk9F4DBocPu5Jrb0

Supplies:
- 2 – 60mm Hoop Earrings
- H/8 – 5mm Crochet Hook
- Worsted Weight cotton
- Darning Needle to sew in ends

Pattern:

ROW 1: SLIP KNOT ONTO HOOP
2DC, 2HD, 4SC , 2HD, 2DC, 2HD, 4SC, 2HD, 2DC , CH1
SLST

ROW 2: CH7, DC IN 4TH CH OF CH7
{3DC IN THE LOOP, CH2, SLST, CH 2[4X]}
CH3 , SKIP 4 , SLST

REPEAT ROW 2 5 TIMES

CUT WORKING YARN AND WEAVE INTO THE
EARRING. USE FABRIC GLUE OR CLEAR GLUE TO
SECURE IT

IDEAS: you can do this in multi colors using for
example green in row 1 then choose a color for row
two. You can also experiment with the flower shapes
and make it your own!

Shell Hoop Earring

These large statement earrings feature an exquisite shell crochet pattern that forms three gracefully cascading rows outside the hoop.

The use of size 4 weight yarn adds a perfect balance, allowing the earrings to be substantial yet comfortably lightweight, making them ideal for a day at the beach or a night out on the town.

The hoops themselves serve as a versatile frame, providing a captivating contrast to the intricacy of the shells. The combination of the circular form and the organic, shell-inspired pattern creates a harmonious blend of bohemian elegance.

Supplies:

- 2- 4 weight yarn of choice
- 4mm Hoop earrings for Small
- 5mm Hoop earring for large
- 3-5mm crochet hook
- Darning needle

Pattern

ROW 1: SLST , SC 32, AROUND HOOP, CH 3 , TRN

ROW 2: 4DC+TOG , 5 LOOPS ON HOOK PULL THOUGH ALL , CH 3, SC, [6x]

ROW 3: CH 5, SC PRE SC, REP TO END , CH 1, TRN

ROW 4: SC IN SAME SPACE, 7 DC IN PREVIOUS SC [5x]

ROW 5: CH 7, TRN, SC IN PREVIOUS SC, REP TO END, CH 1 , TRN

ROW 6: SC IN SAME SPACE, 7SC IN SC, [4x], CUT YARN SLST , THREAD YARN INTO PROJECT

Chandelier Hoop

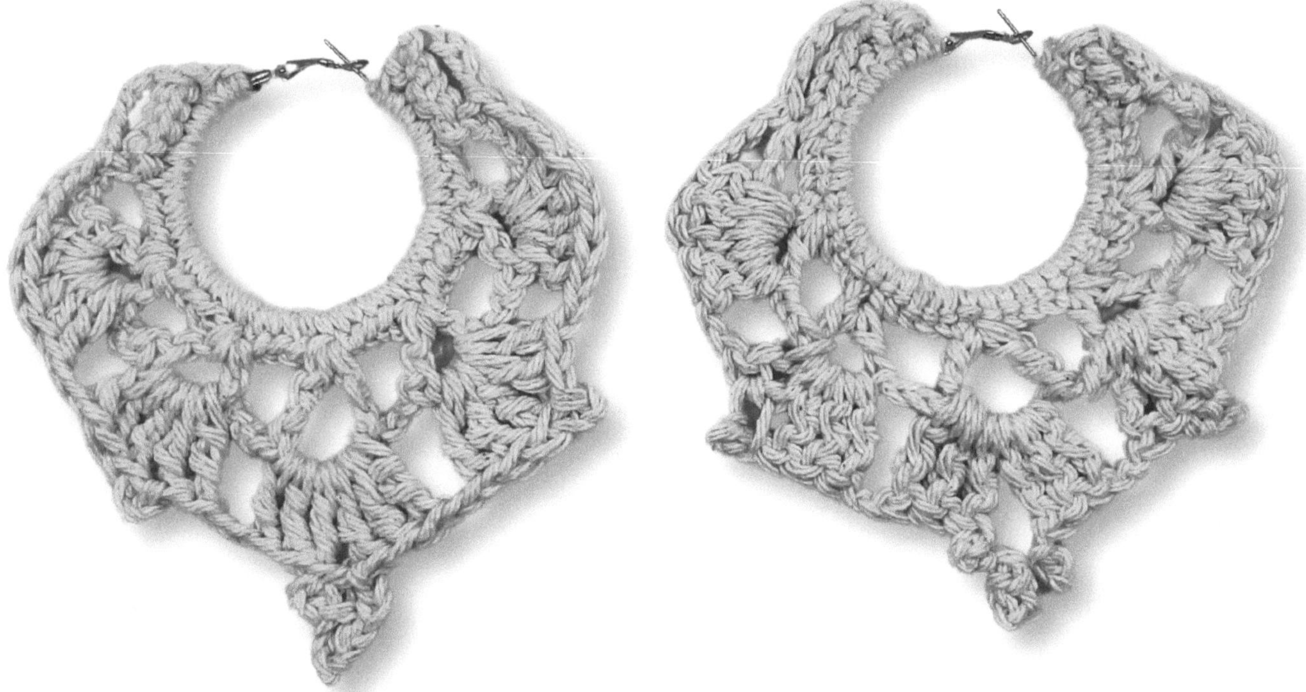

Introducing our captivating handmade crochet hoop earrings, meticulously crafted to perfection. These exquisite earrings boast a unique chandelier shape, with three delicate picots adorning each point for added elegance.

Crafted from 100% cotton yarn, these earrings offer both style and comfort, making them ideal for everyday wear. The design fans out, creating a slim profile toward the top and gradually thickening toward the bottom, where the largest picot sits, adding a touch of sophistication to any outfit.

Whether you're looking to elevate your casual attire or add a chic accent to your evening ensemble, our handmade crochet hoop earrings are the perfect choice.

Supplies:

- 2 – 60mm Hoop Earrings
- 3mm Crochet Hook
- Worsted Weight cotton
- Darning Needle

Pattern:

START WITH A SL ST ON THE HOOK

ROW 1: 42SC AROUND HOOP, CH1 TRN

ROW 2: SLST IN 2ND SC, 4SLST
CH4, [1DC, CH2, 1DC] IN 5TH SC
CH3, [1DC, CH2, 1DC] IN 5TH SC
CH3, [1TR, CH3, 1TR] IN 5TH SC
CH3, [1DC, CH2, 1DC] IN 5TH SC **[2X]**
CH4, SLST IN 5TH SC, 5 SLST, CH1 TRN

ROW 3: CH3, SLST IN 1ST CH, CH3, [5DC] IN SPACE
CH2 [2DC, 1TR, CH3 PICOT, 2TR] IN SPACE
CH2 [3TR, CH3 PICOT, CH5 PICOT, CH3
PICOT, 3TR] IN SPACE
CH2 [3TR, CH3 PICOT, 2DC]
CH2 , 5DC , CH3 SLST IN 5TH CH , 4 SLST

CHAPTER 5:
DANGLE TUTORIALS

FLORAL VINE

Envision a pair of chic dangle crochet earrings that effortlessly blend elegance and whimsy. Cascading from an ear hooks, a slender vine with hand crafted crochet flowers takes center stage. The vine extends to create a captivating uneven composition

This intentional arrangement adds a touch of playfulness to the chic design, reminiscent of flowers gently swaying in the breeze..

Floral Vine Video Tutorial

https://youtu.be/Qnb73KIsnCw?si=UjmVqcQoCPS8QyIS

Supplies:

- 2- 4 weight yarn of choice
- Ear hook & jump ring
- 3-5mm crochet hook
- Darning needle

FLOWER 1: [CH 4, DC IN FIRST CHAIN, CH 4, 4 TR4TOG INTO THE RING, CH 4 , SLST , [3X] ,CH 7 REP [2X]

STEM: CH 12 + 4 , DC INTO PREV 4 CHN. RP FLOWER1 [2X]

JUMP RING: ADD THE JUMP RING ONTO THE 7TH CHAIN IN THE MIDDLE OF THE EARRING .

NOTE: What I like about these is you can add as many vines and flowers as you like. make it your own! you can add adornments or change the petals to "puffs, leaves or any shape you desire"

I used 4 weight acrylic yarn but you can apply this pattern to 2 weight for a more delicate lace look. 100% cotton yarn will produce a neater and stiffer appearance . possibilities are endless explore and write down your patterns.

PINEAPPLE TWIST

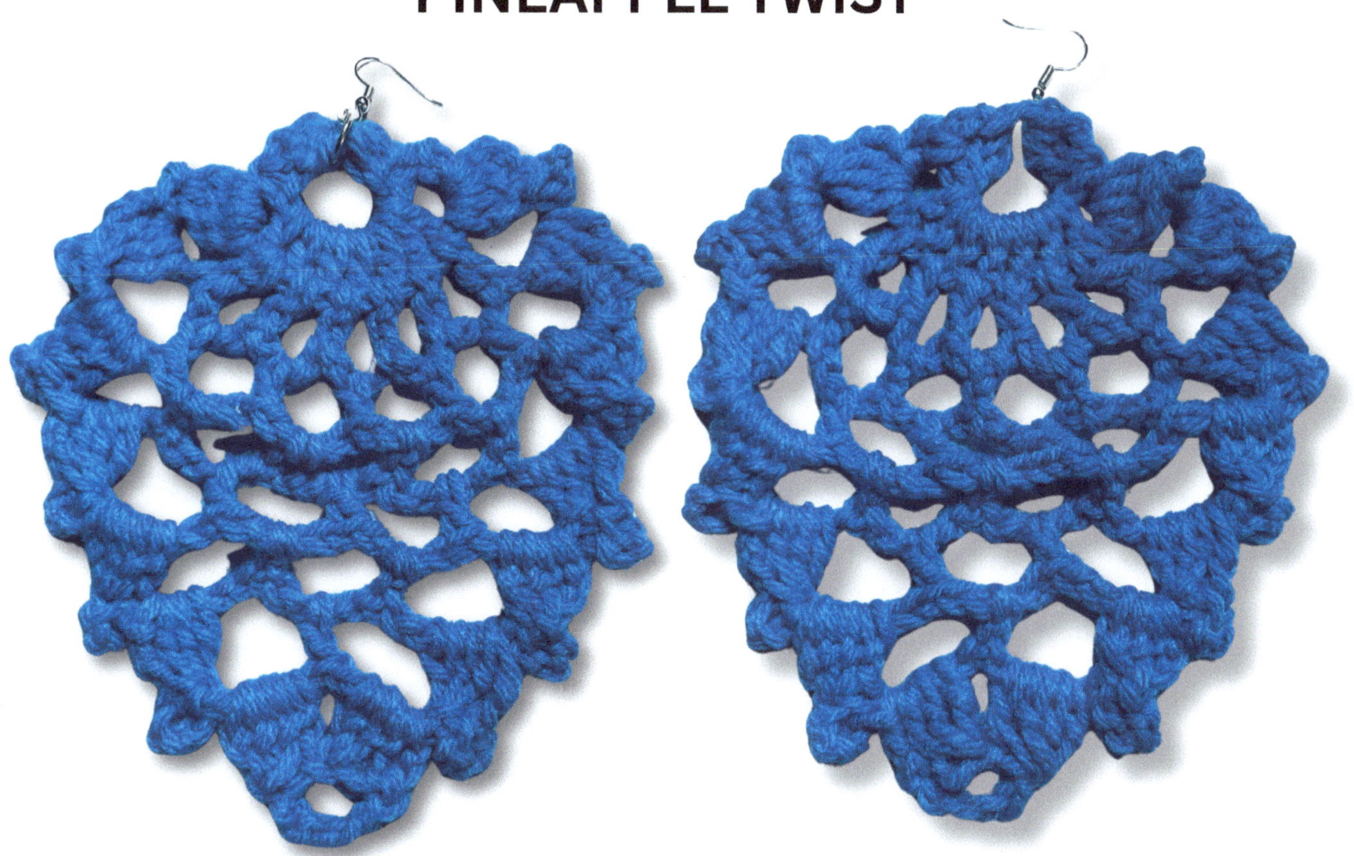

These chic dangle crochet earrings, each adorned with the intricate beauty of the pineapple stitch—a recognizable motif that transforms into a breathtaking vintage-inspired lace design. The pineapple stitch, celebrated for its timeless elegance, takes center stage, creating a cascade of delicate motifs that sway with every movement.

The resulting lacework, reminiscent of a bygone era, forms a motif style that exudes classic charm. The earrings, with their dangling allure, become a wearable piece of art—a fusion of chic contemporary style and vintage elegance. The interplay of light and shadow within the lacework adds depth to the design, creating a visual feast for the eyes.

Supplies:

- 2- 4 weight yarn of choice
- Ear hook & jump ring
- 3-5mm crochet hook
- Darning needle

ROW 1: SLIP KNOT , CH 4 , CL 2DC INTO 1ST CH
PULL THROUGH 3 LOOPS ON HOOK,
CH 5, CL 3DC INTO 1ST CH, CH3, TRN
ROW 2: SLST, 7DC ONTO THE CH 5, CH 1 , CL 3DC IN LAST SPACE
ROW 3: SLST, CHAIN 3 , CL 3CD IN THE SPACE , 3 CH PICOT [CH4, DC] REP 6X
CHN 4, CL 4DC IN LAST SP, 3 CH PICOT
ROW 4: SLST, CH 3, CL 3DC, 3 CH PICOT [CH4 , SC] REP 5X, CHN 4, CL 4DC INTO SP, 4 CH PICOT
ROW 5: SLST, CH 3, CL 3DC, 4 CH PICOT [CH4 , SC] REP 4 X
CHN 4, CL 4DC INTO SP, CH 4 PICOT
ROW 6: SLST, CH 3, CL 3DC4 CH PICOT [CH4 , SC] REP 3 X
CHN 4, CL 4DC INTO SP, CH 5 PICOT
ROW 7: SLST, CH 3, CL 3DC4 CH PICOT [CH4 , SC] REP 2 X
CHN 4, CL 4DC INTO SP, CH 5 PICOT
ROW 8:
SLIP STITCH, CHAIN 3, 3 DOUBLE CROCHET TOGETHER IN THE SPACE 4 DOUBLE CROCHET TOGETHER IN THE LAST SPACE , CHAIN 4
SLIP STITCH INTO THE END

BULLION PUFF CIRCLE

These BOHO circle crochet earrings are skillfully crafted around a central circular hole created by a slip knot, setting the stage for a unique and intricate design. The inner ring of each earring boasts 20 double crochets, forming a solid foundation that contributes to the earrings' stability and structure. Moving outward, the earrings feature an outer ring comprising 20 bullion stitches.

This stitch choice adds a touch of elegance and sophistication, creating a visually interesting contrast with the inner ring. The combination of double crochets, bullion stitches, and the whimsy of the ruffle edge results in a unique accessory that captures the essence of bohemian style while showcasing the versatility of crochet techniques.

BULLION PUFF CIRCLE VIDEO TUTORIAL

https://youtu.be/ZZTAUoMOpmE?si=55mPZkrsWdycx71E

Supplies:

- 4 weight yarn of choice
- Ear hook & jump rings
- 4mm crochet hook
- Darning needle

ROUND 1: MAGIC KNOT, 20DC AROUND RING, CHN2, TIGHTEN MAGIC KNOT , TRN

ROUND 2: 1SC + CH1 [20X], CHN3 TRN

ROUND 3: BULLION STITCH, CH1, 1DC [20X]

"tape 2 hooks together with the hooks opposite of each other. The end of one hook should almost be enough space to catch the yarn. Wrap 6 loops around the two hooks. Insert in the next space and pull through. Then slide the yarn over through the loops."

ROUND 4: 1SC, CH3, 1SC BETWEEN THE BULLION PUFFS,

"MAKE ONE SC ON THE RIGHT OF THE DC , CHAIN 3 AND MAKE ONE SC ON THE LEFT OF THE DC. REPEAT

[20X]

TASSEL DOILY

In the heart of each earring lies a circular motif, echoing the timeless elegance of doilies. The inner circle serves as a canvas for the subsequent artistry, providing a foundation for the unfolding pattern that follows.

At each end of the ovals, dainty picots make their appearance, like small flourishes that add a playful and whimsical touch to the overall composition. The picots contribute to the sense of delicacy and femininity, transforming the earrings into more than just accessories—they become wearable pieces of art.

TASSEL EARRING TUTORIAL

https://youtu.be/fGkFS5wVPP4?si=svKaD8LQJ45JpH9p

Supplies:

- 2- 4 weight yarn of choice
- Ear hook & jump ring
- 3-5mm crochet hook
- Darning needle

FOUNDATION: SLIP KNOT, CH 10, SLST

ROUND 1: CH1, TRN, 20 SC INTO SPACE

ROUND 2: CH6, DC INTO SAME STITCH
- CH3, SK 1, DC , REP 5X
- CH 3, DC IN SAME STITCH
- CH 3,SK 1, DC, REP 4X , SLST INTO 3RD STITCH IN THE FOLLOWING CH

ROUND 3: CH 1 , SC, HDC, DC + 3 CH PICOT, DC, HDC, SC IN 1ST SPACE
- SC, HDC, CH 1, HDC, SC IN THE NEXT 4 SPACES
- SC, HDC, DC + 3 CH PICOT, DC, HDC, SC
- SC, HDC, CH 1, HDC, SC IN THE NEXT 4 SPACES SLST TO FINISH THE PROJECT.

TASSEL: WRAP YARN AROUND YOUR FINGERS AT-LEAST 10 TIMES . INSERT THE JUMP RING AT THE TOP PART OF YOUT LOOPS AND CUT THE END, THEN WRAP AROUND UNDER THE JUMP RING AND TIE IT OFF WITH A FEW KNOTS . CUT YOUR BOTTOM HOOPS AND TRIM TO YOUR DESIRED LENGTH.

LEAF - TUNISIAN CROCHET

Envision a pair of captivating BOHO LEAF TUNISIAN crochet earrings, each suspended delicately from an open bezel. These unique earrings are a celebration of nature-inspired artistry, capturing the essence of bohemian beauty and the intricate allure of Tunisian crochet.

The focal point of these earrings is the intricately crafted leaf motif that gracefully hangs from the open bezel. The leaf design, inspired by nature's elegance, features detailed veins and contours, creating a visual tapestry reminiscent of a bohemian basket weave. The interplay of stitches forms a rich texture that evokes the organic and free-spirited essence of bohemian style.

TUNISIAN LEAF VIDEO TUTORIAL

https://youtu.be/_ErTJB4nQNI?si=RBHkfxWZjATPVILb

Supplies:

- 2- 4 weight yarn of choice
- Small round open bezel or key-chain
- Ear hook & jump ring
- 4mm Tunisian crochet hook
- Darning needle

PATTERN:

- BEGIN WITH A SLIP KNOT AND SC ONTO THE OPEN BEZEL , CHN 1 , PULL UP 2ND LOOP UNDER THE CHN 1, SC FROM INSIDE THE BEZEL , SC INTO LEFT OVER LOOP

- PULL UP LOOP FROM UNDER SC, PULL UP 3RD LOOP FROM PREVIOUS SC , SC FROM INSIDE OPEN BEZEL, SC NEXT 2 LOOPS

- REPEAT UNTIL DESIRED LENGTH , CUT OFF AND FASTEN THE TAIL

-

TIP: THIS CROCHET PATTERN WILL RETAIN ITS SHAPE THE LONGER YOU MAKE THE EARRING ON ITS OWN. YOU WILL START TO SEE STRAIGHT LINES FORMING . THIS IS HOW YOU WILL KEEP TRACK OF THE NUMBER OF LAYERS YOUR OWN AS WELL AS THE SPACE TO PULL UP YOUR LOOPS. ITS LAYER SHOULD GROW BY ONE SINGLE CROCHET

CHAPTER 6:
Finishing Techniques

Blocking and Shaping

Blocking and shaping are essential finishing techniques in crochet that enhance the overall appearance and structure of your projects. Whether you've completed a delicate lace shawl or a cozy blanket, blocking helps to even out stitches, open up lacework, and give your project a polished, professional look. Here are tips and instructions on crochet blocking and shaping:

Blocking

Wet Blocking:
1. Prepare Your Project:
   - Finish crocheting your project and weave in all ends.

2. Fill a Basin with Water:
   - Fill a basin or sink with lukewarm water.

3. Add a Mild Detergent:
   - Optionally, add a small amount of mild detergent to the water if your yarn is machine washable.

4. Submerge Your Project:
   - Gently submerge your crochet project in the water, ensuring it is fully saturated.

5. Soak for 15-20 Minutes:
   - Allow your project to soak for 15-20 minutes to relax the fibers.

6. Drain and Gently Squeeze Out Excess Water:
   - Drain the water and gently squeeze out excess water from your project.

7. Lay Out on Blocking Mats or Towels:
   - Lay your project flat on blocking mats or towels, shaping it to the desired dimensions.

8. Pin in Place:
   - Use rust proof pins to pin your project into the desired shape, paying attention to edges and corners.

9. Leave to Dry Completely:
   - Allow your project to dry completely before unpinning. This might take a day or more depending on the yarn and the project's size.

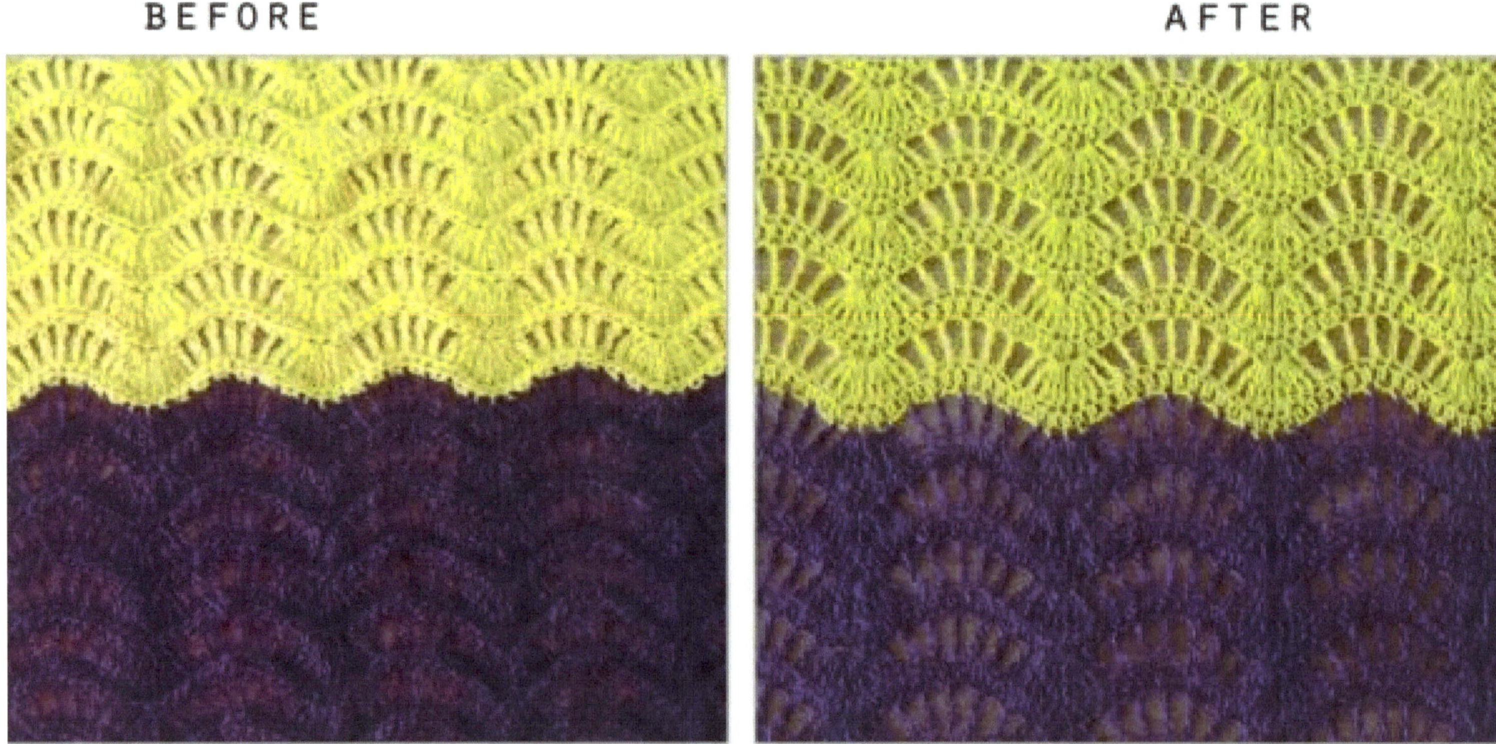

Steam Blocking:

1. Prepare Your Project:
   - Finish crocheting your project and weave in all ends.

2. Lay Project Flat:
   - Lay your project flat on a blocking surface.

3. Hold a Steaming Iron Above Your Project:
   - Hold a steaming iron about 1-2 inches above your project, releasing bursts of steam.

4. Gently Shape and Stretch:
   - While steaming, gently shape and stretch your project to the desired dimensions.

5. Leave to Cool and Dry:
   - Allow your project to cool and dry completely before moving or wearing it.

Shaping:

1. Consider the Fiber:
   - Different fibers respond differently to blocking. Natural fibers like wool can be blocked more aggressively than synthetic fibers.

2. Check the Pattern:
   - Refer to the pattern instructions for specific blocking recommendations. Some projects may require aggressive blocking for lacework, while others may need a more subtle approach.

3. Measure as You Go:
   - Use a tape measure to ensure that your project is blocked to the correct dimensions as you pin it in place.

4. Block with Intent:
   - Pay attention to details like edges, corners, and stitch patterns. Shape your project with the final result in mind.

5. Use Blocking Wires:
   - Blocking wires can help you achieve straight edges in larger projects, such as shawls or blankets.

6. Block Accessories Too:
   - Don't forget to block accessories like hats or gloves. This ensures a proper fit and a polished finish.

7. Experiment with Tension:
   - Adjust the tension in your blocking to achieve different effects. Light tension can subtly shape, while firm tension can dramatically alter the fabric.

8. Be Patient:
   - Allow your project to dry completely before unpinning. This is crucial for maintaining the blocked shape.

Adding Earring Findings

Adding earring findings to crochet earrings is the final step in completing your beautiful accessory. Whether you've created intricate lace earrings or cute amigurumi character earrings, properly attaching findings ensures a secure and polished finish. Here's a detailed guide on how to add earring findings to crochet earrings.

 Materials Needed:

1. Completed Crochet Earrings:
   - Ensure your crochet earrings are fully finished, with all ends woven in.

2. Earring Findings:
   - Choose the style of earring findings you prefer, such as hooks, studs, or clips. Ensure they match the design and size of your earrings.

3. Jump Rings (if needed):
   - Depending on your earring design, you may need jump rings to attach the findings to your crochet earrings.

4. Needle and Thread (optional):
   - A small amount of matching thread can be used for added security.

Instructions:

For Earring Hooks:

1. Open the Loop:
   - If your earring hook has a loop, use pliers to gently open it.

2. Insert the Earring:
   - Insert the loop through the designated stitch or space on your crochet earring.

3. Close the Loop:
   - Use pliers to close the loop securely. Ensure it is closed tightly to prevent the earring from slipping off

For Stud Earrings:

1. Attach Stud Earring Blank:
   - If your stud earrings have a blank (flat metal surface), use strong glue to attach the blank to the back of your crochet earring.

2. Secure with Thread (optional):
   - For added security, you can use a needle and thread to stitch the blank to the crochet earring. This is especially useful for heavier earrings.

For Clip-On Earrings:

1. Attach Clip-On Finding:
   - Open the clip-on finding and attach it to the back of your crochet earring.

2. Secure with Thread (optional):
   - Similar to stud earrings, you can use a needle and thread to stitch the clip-on finding to the crochet earring for additional support.

For Dangle Earrings with Jump Rings:

1. Add Jump Rings:
   - If your design includes dangle elements, attach jump rings to the crochet earring where you want the dangles to hang.

2. Attach Earring Hook or Stud:
   - Use additional jump rings to attach the earring hook or stud to the jump ring on your crochet earring.

3. Secure with Thread (optional):
   - If your earrings have movement or weight, consider using a needle and thread to reinforce the connections.

Tips:

1. Choose Appropriate Findings:
   - Ensure the earring findings you choose match the style, size, and weight of your crochet earrings.
2. Use Quality Materials:
   - Invest in quality earring findings to ensure durability and prevent allergies.
3. Consider Weight:
   - If your earrings are heavier, opt for findings with secure closures or reinforce with additional thread.
4. Test the Strength:
   - Before wearing or selling, test the strength of the attachments to ensure the earrings are secure.
5. Be Mindful of Allergies:
   - If you or your intended recipient has metal allergies, choose hypoallergenic findings.
6. Maintain Consistency:
   - Ensure both earrings have findings attached at the same point for a professional finish.
7. Customize with Beads or Charms:
   - Add beads or charms to the findings for extra embellishment and personalization.

Securing Ends and Weaving in Yarn Tails

Securing ends and weaving in yarn tails is a crucial step in completing your crochet projects. Properly securing and hiding yarn ends ensures a polished and professional finish, preventing your hard work from unraveling over time. Here's a detailed guide on how to secure ends and weave in yarn tails in crochet:

Materials Needed:
1. Completed Crochet Project:
   - Ensure your crochet project is complete, with no more stitches to be added.

2. Darning Needle:
   - Use a blunt-tip yarn needle with a large eye for ease of threading.

Instructions:

For Fastening Off:
1. Cut Yarn:
   - After completing the final stitch of your project, cut the yarn, leaving a tail of about 4-6 inches.

2. Yarn Over and Pull Through:
   - Yarn over and pull the cut end through the last loop on the hook.

3. Pull Tight:
   - Pull the cut end tight to secure the last stitch.

For Weaving in Ends:
1. Thread the Yarn Needle:
   - Thread the cut end of the yarn through the eye of the yarn needle.

2. Weave Through Stitches:
   - Insert the needle into the back of the nearest stitch, working in the same direction as the stitches.

3. Weave Through a Few Stitches:
   - Weave the yarn through several stitches in one direction. This helps anchor the yarn securely.

4. Change Direction:
   - Turn and weave the yarn back through the stitches in the opposite direction. This creates a woven pattern that secures the yarn.

5. Trim Excess:
   - Trim any excess yarn, leaving a small tail that is securely woven into the stitches.

For Joining New Yarn:
1. Leave a Tail:
   - When joining a new yarn color or skein, leave a tail of about 4-6 inches.

2. Hold the Tail Alongside the Stitches:
   - Hold the tail of the new yarn alongside the stitches as you work the next few stitches. This helps secure the tail.

3. Weave in the Tail:
   - After working a few stitches, thread the tail through the yarn needle and weave it into the stitches in the same manner as described above.

4. Trim Excess:
   - Trim any excess yarn, leaving a small tail that is securely woven into the stitches.

Tips:

1. Weave in as You Go:
   - Whenever possible, weave in yarn tails as you work on your project. This reduces the number of tails to weave in at the end.

2. Match Yarn Colors:
   - When joining a new color, choose a yarn tail that matches the color of the stitches you are working with.

3. Weave into Similar-Colored Stitches:
   - Weave the yarn tail into stitches that are similar in color to the yarn tail. This helps hide the tail within the fabric.

4. Avoid Weaving in Tight Stitches:
   - Choose looser stitches or gaps between stitches for weaving in yarn tails. This ensures flexibility and prevents puckering.

5. Don't Overstretch:
   - Avoid pulling the yarn too tight when weaving in ends, as this can distort the stitches.

6. Secure at Seams:
   - If your project has seams, weave in ends along the seam lines for added reinforcement.

7. Check After Washing:
   - After washing your project, check the woven-in ends to ensure they are still secure. Re-weave if necessary.

By following these instructions and tips, you'll achieve a clean and professional finish for your crochet projects. Properly securing ends and weaving in yarn tails ensures the longevity and durability of your work, leaving you with a polished and well-crafted final product.

Troubleshooting Crochet Tension
Achieving proper tension is crucial in crochet, as it directly affects the appearance and drape of your projects. Tension refers to the tightness or looseness with which you work the yarn while crocheting. In this chapter, we'll delve into common tension issues and introduce three tension categories: Yankers, Riders, and Lifters. When I first started I discovered I'm a yanker. I was stitching too tightly which can lead to curling and difficulty entering loops. Which type are you?

Understanding Crochet Tension:

Proper Tension:
Achieving consistent tension ensures that your stitches are uniform, creating a polished and professional-looking project. Proper tension is a balance between not too tight and not too loose, allowing the yarn to flow smoothly.

Common Tension Issues:
1. Too Tight (Yankers)
   - Symptoms: Stitches are compact, and the fabric feels stiff. It can be challenging to insert the hook into stitches.
   - Causes:
   - Tensioning the yarn too tightly while holding the working yarn.
   - Holding the crochet hook too tightly.
   - Solution:
   - Relax your grip on both the yarn and the crochet hook.
 - Focus on maintaining a consistent, gentle tension as you work.

2. Too Loose (Riders):
   - Symptoms: Stitches are overly large and lack definition. The fabric may appear floppy.
   - Causes:
   - Insufficient tension on the yarn while crocheting.
   - Not maintaining a consistent tension throughout the project.
   - Solution:
   - Tighten your grip slightly on both the yarn and the crochet hook.
   - Pay attention to keeping a steady tension as you crochet.

3. Inconsistent Tension (Lifters):
   - Symptoms: Uneven stitches, with some tight and others loose. The fabric may look uneven and lack cohesion.
   - Causes:
   - Tension varies unintentionally while working.
   - Changes in hand position or technique during crocheting.
   - Solution:
   - Practice maintaining a steady tension by focusing on a specific hand position.
   - Be mindful of changes in your grip or technique that might affect tension.

Tips for Troubleshooting Tension:

1. Practice Swatches:
   - Create tension swatches before starting a project to ensure your tension is consistent.

2. Relax Your Hands:
   - Keep your hands and fingers relaxed. Tension issues often stem from unnecessary tension in the hands.

3. Experiment with Hook Sizes:
   - If you notice consistent tension issues, try using a different crochet hook size. Some individuals naturally achieve better tension with larger or smaller hooks.

4. Use Yarn Guides:
   - Yarn guides, such as tension rings or yarn thimbles, can help regulate yarn tension by providing a consistent point of contact.

5. Check Your Posture:
   - Maintain good posture while crocheting. Poor posture can lead to hand fatigue and unintentional changes in tension.

6. Take Breaks:
   - If you find yourself becoming tense or fatigued, take short breaks to relax your hands and prevent tension issues.

7. Adjusting Mid-Project:
   - If you notice tension changes during a project, it's okay to unravel a few stitches and adjust your tension before continuing.

Remember that achieving consistent tension is a skill that develops over time with practice. Don't be discouraged by initial challenges, and experiment with different techniques until you find what works best for you. With patience and attention, you'll master the art of maintaining proper tension in your crochet projects.

Dealing with yarn splitting
Dealing with yarn splitting and fraying can be a common challenge in crochet, but there are several tips and ideas to help you overcome these issues and create smoother, more enjoyable stitching experiences. Here are some helpful tips:

Tips for Dealing with Yarn Splitting:
1. Choose Smooth Yarn:
   - Opt for yarns with a smooth texture rather than ones with a loose or fuzzy structure. Smooth yarns are less likely to split.

2. Use a Smaller Hook:
   - If you notice consistent splitting, try using a slightly smaller crochet hook. This can help you catch all the strands of the yarn without splitting it.

3. Be Mindful of Yarn Composition:
   - Yarns with multiple plies may be more prone to splitting. Consider using single-ply or fewer-plied yarns for projects where splitting is a concern.

4. Avoid Dull or Rough Hooks:
   - Ensure your crochet hook is in good condition. Dull or rough hooks can catch and split the yarn. Consider using a polished or coated hook for smoother stitching.

5. Crochet with Consistent Tension:
   - Maintain a consistent tension while crocheting to minimize the risk of splitting. Uneven tension can lead to the hook piercing through the yarn strands.

6. Be Gentle:
   - Crochet gently and avoid forcing the hook through the yarn. A gentle and controlled approach can help prevent splitting.

7. Use a Yarn Guide:
   - Consider using a yarn guide on your finger to control the yarn tension and reduce the chances of splitting.

Tips for Dealing with Yarn Fraying:

1. Choose Quality Yarn:
   - Invest in high-quality yarns that are less likely to fray. Quality fibers and construction can make a significant difference.

2. Store Yarn Properly:
   - Store your yarn in a cool, dry place to prevent it from becoming brittle and prone to fraying.

3. Avoid Overhandling:
   - Minimize excessive handling of the yarn, especially if it's a delicate or loosely spun fiber. Overhandling can contribute to fraying.

4. Use a Yarn Holder or Bowl:
   - Place your yarn in a yarn holder or bowl to reduce friction and prevent excessive movement that may cause fraying.

5. Check Your Hook for Burrs:
   - Inspect your crochet hook regularly for any burrs or rough spots that could contribute to yarn fraying. Smooth out any imperfections with fine sandpaper or a nail file.

6. Be Careful with Joining Techniques:
   - Pay attention to how you join new yarn or change colors. If not done properly, it can lead to fraying. Consider using knotless joining methods or weaving in ends carefully.

7. Block and Finish Carefully:
   - Block your finished projects gently to prevent unnecessary stress on the yarn. Finish off and weave in ends carefully to avoid any unraveling.

8. Use a Yarn Wax or Conditioner:
   - Applying a small amount of yarn wax or conditioner can reduce friction and make the yarn more resistant to fraying.

Remember that different yarns may have unique characteristics, and it's essential to adapt your techniques based on the specific yarn you're using. By being mindful of your materials and adjusting your approach, you can minimize issues related to yarn splitting and fraying, allowing you to enjoy your crochet projects with ease.

Adjusting patterns for different yarn weights
Adjusting crochet patterns for different yarn weights is a useful skill that allows you to customize projects to your preferred yarn or to use up your existing yarn stash. Here are instructions and tips on how to adjust crochet patterns for different yarn weights:

Instructions:

1. Understand the Original Pattern:
   - Begin by thoroughly reading the original pattern. Understand the stitch count, gauge, and any special instructions.

2. Choose Your Yarn:
   - Select a yarn of your desired weight that is suitable for the project. Pay attention to the recommended hook size on the yarn label.

3. Check Gauge:
   - Crochet a gauge swatch using the new yarn and hook to ensure that your stitches match the pattern's gauge. Adjust the hook size if necessary.

4. Calculate the Ratio:
   - Compare the gauge of your swatch with the pattern's gauge. Calculate the ratio between the two gauges to determine how many stitches and rows you need to adjust.
   $$ Ratio = (Your Gauge Stitches per Inch / Pattern Gauge Stitches per Inch) \times Original Stitch Count $$
   - Repeat the calculation for rows if needed.

5. Adjust Stitch Count:
   - Multiply each stitch count in the pattern by the calculated ratio to adjust the number of stitches. Round to the nearest whole number.

6. Adjust Row Count:
   - If needed, repeat the process for rows by multiplying each row count in the pattern by the calculated ratio.

7. Modify Stitch Patterns:
   - Be aware that certain stitch patterns or motifs may need additional adjustments. Ensure that pattern repeats align correctly.

8. Consider Sizing:
   - If you're adjusting a garment, check the sizing information in the pattern. Make sure that your new stitch and row counts align with the desired size.

9. Maintain Proportions:
   - Maintain the proportions of the original pattern. If the pattern has specific stitch multiples or repeat counts, adjust them accordingly to keep the design balanced.

10. Adjust Hook Size:
 - If your new yarn creates a fabric that is too stiff or too loose, consider adjusting the hook size to achieve the desired drape.

11. Check Yardage:
 - Be aware that changing yarn weight may affect the amount of yarn needed. Check the yardage requirements in the pattern and adjust accordingly.

Tips:

1. Save a Swatch:
   - Keep a swatch of your adjusted gauge as a reference for future projects using the same yarn weight.

2. Write It Down:
   - Document your adjustments on the pattern or in a notebook to avoid confusion and make it easier to recreate the project.

3. Experiment with Samples:
   - If you're unsure about the adjustments, create a small sample of the pattern to test your changes before committing to the full project.

4. Consider Yarn Substitutes:
   - If the exact yarn weight is unavailable, consider using a yarn with a similar fiber content and thickness.

5. Use Online Calculators:
   - There are online calculators that can help you adjust stitch counts and gauge. Input your original and desired gauge to get the adjusted stitch count.

6. Be Flexible:
   - Be open to experimenting and adjusting as you go. Crochet is a creative process, and sometimes a bit of trial and error is involved.
By following these instructions and tips, you'll be able to confidently adjust crochet patterns for different yarn weights, opening up a world of possibilities for customizing your projects.

Closing

In closing, congratulations on completing this crochet tutorial book! I hope these pages have been a source of inspiration, guidance, and joy in your creative journey. As you've explored the various chapters, learned new techniques, and embarked on beautiful projects, remember that the world of crochet is boundless, with endless possibilities waiting to be discovered.

As you continue your crochet adventures beyond these pages, I encourage you to share your creations, connect with fellow enthusiasts, and revel in the supportive and vibrant crochet community. Also follow and share on my social media @artesmess . Remember that each project is an opportunity to learn, grow, and express yourself through the art of crochet.

May your yarn be ever soft, your stitches ever even, and your projects filled with love. Whether you're crafting cozy blankets, stylish wearables, or delicate accessories, savor the meditative moments and the satisfaction of turning a skein of yarn into a tangible work of art.

Thank you for allowing Artes'mss to be part of your journey through this book. Wishing you countless hours of joy, creativity, and fulfillment as you continue to explore the endless possibilities that crochet has to offer. Happy crocheting!

THE END

ACKNOWLEDGEMENTS

I want to thank everyone who has encouraged my artistic talent ! Anyone who has like, shared or purchased my earrings!

Special Thank you to Amore Ayala of Sew Style Hause for investing in my book and for all the ideas you poured into this book. You are a true gem I wouldn't have thought about writing a book until I saw how easy it was for you to do!

to my late mother Stacey Bell who has supported me in everything and to and to whom I get my artistic talent from. to my Grandmother Dosher who I learned crafting from she can turn anything into decor, my dad Eddie and my many sisters for the support !

To my friends who have worn my pieces and purchased art I am grateful Tiffany, Ralphie, Jaya, Ghizel, Ray Rahim Brazil, Janay, Carla, Joshlyn, Johnathan. Cousins Doris , Octavia , Sierra ! sorry if I missed anyone !

Redris